Ann Andrews ar
the Birmingham
Money Advice C
have great exp
with debt proble
to show a wider
them.

Ann Andrews is a barrister and has worked at
the Birmingham Settlement for four years on the
Money Advice Project, as a case officer. She
chairs the Money Advice Association and has
lectured to numerous groups in this field.

Peter Houghton is the Director of the Birming-
ham Settlement and pioneered the Money
Advice Centre. He is also the author of COPING
WITH CHILDLESSNESS (George Allen &
Unwin).

The HOW TO Series

HOW TO COPE WITH CREDIT AND DEAL WITH DEBT –
Ann Andrews and Peter Houghton
HOW TO FACE THE INTERVIEW –
Clive Fletcher
HOW TO PASS EXAMS –
Fred Orr
HOW TO SPLIT UP AND SURVIVE FINANCIALLY –
Tony Hetherington

How to Cope with Credit and Deal with Debt

ANN ANDREWS and
PETER HOUGHTON

London
UNWIN PAPERBACKS
Boston   Sydney

First published by Unwin Paperbacks 1986

UNWIN® PAPERBACKS
40 Museum Street, London WC1A 1LU, UK

Unwin Paperbacks
Park Lane, Hemel Hempstead, Herts HP2 4TE, UK

George Allen & Unwin Australia Pty Ltd
8 Napier Street, North Sydney, NSW 2060, Australia

Unwin Paperbacks with the
Port Nicholson Press
PO Box 11–838 Wellington, New Zealand

ISBN 0–04–346002 X

Set in 10 on 11 point Palatino by Bedford Typesetters Ltd, Bedford,
and printed in Great Britain by Cox and Wyman Ltd, Reading

Contents

Acknowledgements   *page* xi

1   The Onset of Debt   1

Causes of Debt   3
   Loss of income   3
   Increase in expenditure   5
   Over-commitment   7
Consequences of Indebtedness   8
Steps in the Debt Experience   9
   One family's experience of debt   10
Who Is to Blame for Debt?   16

2   Using Credit   18

What Is Credit?   18
Ways of Obtaining Credit   20
   Fixed-term v revolving credit   20
   Secured v unsecured credit   21
   Credit-granters and types of credit   21
Choosing the Right Type of Credit   27
   The cost of credit   28
   The repayment term   31
   The repayments required   31
   The method of repayment   33
   The reputation of the credit-granter   33
   The consequences if default occurs   34
   Convenience   35
   Can you afford it?   35
Who Gets the Credit   36
   Credit-scoring   36
   Credit-reference agency   37
   Personal experience/interview   37
   Red-lining   38

Insurance   *page* 39
Consumer Credit Protection   39
  The agreement   40
  Extortionate credit   42
  Rebate for early settlement   42
  Duty to give information   43
Loan Sharks   43
Miscellaneous Points on Using Credit   44
  Guaranteeing a credit agreement   44
  Joint liability for credit/debts   44
  Death of a borrower   45
Credit Unions   45
Conclusion   46

3 The Creditor's Experience of Debt   48

The Creditor's Rights when Default Occurs   49
Creditor's Steps after Default   52
  Head office – computerised letter   53
  Branch office – letters, telephone calls, visits   54
  Door-to-door collection   56
  Passing the debt to a solicitor   56
  Passing the debt to a debt collection agency   57
  Selling the debt to a debt collector   57
  Court proceedings   57
Harassment   58
Complaints about Creditors or Debt Collectors   60
Conclusion   61

4 Debt Control – What to do to Start to Help Yourself   62

Being Realistic   62
Income   63
  The Andersons   64
Regular Expenditure   65
  The Andersons   65
Irregular Expenditure   67
  The Andersons   68
Solutions Debtors Often Try   71
  Commercial borrowing   72
  Borrowing from family and friends   73
  Selling an asset   74
  Cashing insurance policies   75
  Robbing Peter to pay Paul   75

Disappearing *page* 75
Buying time with creditors 76
The Systematic Approach 76
The importance of the Financial Statement 77

5 Maximising Your Income 78

Increasing Your Household's Earnings 79
Income tax – are you paying too much? 79
Low wages 82
Part-time work 84
Partner's earnings 84
State Benefits 85
Family Income Supplement 86
Housing Benefit 86
Supplementary Benefit 87
Other social security benefits 89
Income from Other Members of
Your Household 90
Lodgers 90
Non-dependants 91
Separation and Divorce 93
Income tax 93
Irregular maintenance 94
Child Benefit 96
Miscellaneous Points 96
Staff welfare funds 96
Charities 96
Selling an asset 97
Cashing insurance policies 97
Contributions from friends or relatives 97
Education grants 97
Special Cases 98
Students 98
The disabled and elderly 98
Casual earnings – the black economy 99
Checklist 100
The Andersons 101

6 Essential Outgoings 103

Dividing Your Expenditure into Four
Categories 104
Category 1 – Basic Essentials Easy to Quantify 105
Housekeeping 106

Insurance   *page* 107
Travelling expenses   107
Television   108
How to pay   108
The Andersons   111
Category 2 – Essential Items Difficult to
Quantify   112
Clothing   112
Repairs and replacements   113
School expenses   113
Health expenses   113
Entertainment, birthdays, Christmas, toys and
books   113
Budgeting for Category 2   114
The Andersons   114
Category 3 – The Extras That Make Life
Worthwhile   115
Cigarettes, alcohol, gambling   116
Holidays   117
Video rental   117
Telephone   117
The Andersons   118
Category 4 – Credit Commitments   119
Living on Benefit   119

7 Priority Debts   121

Two Vital Points   121
Listing Your Debts   122
Choosing Your Priorities   123
Mortgage arrears   123
Rent arrears   130
Rates arrears   132
Water rates arrears   135
Fuel debts   136
Fines   142
Maintenance arrears   144
Hire purchase payments and arrears   146
Priority debts for the self-employed   147
More Than One Priority Debt   147
Priority Debts – No Disposable Income   149
Conclusion   149

8 Unsecured Debts   151

The Facts You Need   152

Drafting a Repayment Programme   *page* 156
The Negotiations   161
    All creditors accept   162
    All creditors refuse   162
    Some creditors refuse   163
    A majority accept   163
    A creditor refuses to suspend interest   163
    A creditor refuses to accept despite all your efforts 166
Persuading Creditors to Cooperate   167
Some Points on Payment   169
Long-term Consequences of Reducing
Payments   170
What to Do if There Is No Disposable
Income for Unsecured Creditors   171
Getting Debts 'Written off'   172
Debts to Relatives   174
Conclusion   174

9   Using the Courts and Bankruptcy   175

Your Feelings about Courts   176
General Principles in Court   177
The System in England and Wales   178
    Possession proceedings: rent arrears/
    secured loan arrears/mortgage arrears   179
    Hire purchase proceedings   182
    Unsecured debts   184
    Administration orders   190
    Time orders   193
The System in Northern Ireland   196
    Unsecured debts   196
The System in Scotland   199
    Unsecured debts   200
    Rates arrears   204
    Fines   205
Bankruptcy   205
    Discharge from bankruptcy   207
Conclusion   207

10 The Need for Reform   209

Changing the Atmosphere   209
A New Approach to Default   211
    A national money advice service   211

A national borrowers' league   *page* 211
Improvements in creditors' procedures   212
Poverty and Debt   213
Reform of the Courts   215
Responsible Lending   216
A national credit register   217

Self-Help Kit   219

Further Reading   227

Index   228

Acknowledgements

We have written this book because of our experiences of giving advice to people with debt problems. Most people with financial problems do not have, and cannot afford, access to the expert professional advice they need. They are also often seen as letting the side down. In this book we try to explain how easy it is to fall into financial difficulty in today's society that invites us to live on credit. We hope we have set out for borrowers a way in which they can be their own professional expert in tackling any money problems they may have.

Our thanks must go first of all to the clients of the Birmingham Settlement Money Advice Centre, who for the last fifteen years have shared their problems with us, and some of whose stories are in this book. We must also thank those at the Settlement who developed debt counselling as a skill and defined the techniques described here. In this John Blamire was a leading pioneer.

Thanks must also go to those enlightened creditors who have referred some of their troubled borrowers to us and who have been willing to negotiate with us.

Finally, thanks to those who advised us and sustained us in writing the book – to Peter Andrews, Diane Houghton, Nicola Thomas, Patrick Conaty, Pat Moran, Anthony Harris, Roger Otto, Jemmial Bennison, and the Castlemilk Law Centre Glasgow, for help with the text and style of presentation, also to Tim Marren and Stephen Wheldon for their work in preparing the index. And last, but by no means least, to Ann Lane for typing uncomplainingly from our many drafts and corrections.

How to Cope with Credit and Deal with Debt

1

The Onset of Debt

If you have taken this book off the shelf, you are probably worried about a money matter. It may be your own problem or that of a relative or friend. You may remember difficult times, now happily past, but want to avoid them in future. You may just feel a sense of being over-committed, of having too little money left when trying to pay your weekly or monthly commitments. If you have these feelings, you are a typical member of the credit society.

* Over 60 per cent of us purchase our homes on credit through a mortgage.

* Over 90 per cent of us purchase our fuel on credit, by quarterly account.

* We borrow a massive £19,000 million each year to finance our consumer credit purchases.

* One-third of all consumer items are purchased on credit.

* It is estimated that together we owe £27,000 million to the banks, finance houses and other money lenders for predominantly consumer purchases.

The majority of us owe others money, but that does not make us 'debtors'; we are 'credit-users'. You are not a debtor unless you have failed to meet a commitment or pay a bill at the time it is due. However, credit can quickly turn into debt. This happens to many ordinary people every year.

* Each year nearly 2 million county court actions are commenced against people who owe money, who have been unable to pay their way, and whose creditors have taken them to court.

* Each year 1½ million electricity consumers and 1 million gas consumers have difficulty paying their bills, and over 140,000 households find themselves disconnected from their fuel supply.

* Nationwide, 25 per cent of local authority tenants are in arrears with their rent, and house repossession due to mortgage arrears is increasing. It is estimated that building societies have 100,000 borrowers more than three months in arrears, and in one large city one-third of local authority mortgages are more than one month in arrears.

You may not be one of these statistics, you may be one of those people the financial institutions call 'credit-worthy'. But if you have pledged part of your future income to someone else by using credit, you are gambling with your future ability to pay. You are relying on being able to maintain your income at least at its present level, and for some of us this will not be a correct expectation.

On the other hand, credit is a good thing. It helps us to buy the things we need in life. Buying a house is considered a good long-term investment, the value of the house rising faster than the mortgage repayments, on which we get tax relief. Any sensible person wants to buy like this. Most of the things we buy, however, lose value immediately after purchase, so we are paying in the future for a less and less valuable object. A car, washing machine, three-piece suite, carpet, clothes, cannot be resold for what we paid for them. Other things such as gas and electricity, which we pay for

THE ONSET OF DEBT

after we have used them, have no resale value at all. So next month's, quarter's, year's, even ten years' income, is already committed in part.

So what, you may say. This is nothing new. The whole point of earning money is to allow us to buy our necessities. We shall always need to owe money, and there is nothing new about the problems people have with money. There have always been people with more than enough, some with too little, the majority with just about enough.

What is new is that more and more people every year are encouraged to take the 'waiting out of wanting', to 'buy now – pay later'. A finance company representative looking at his default figures, commented 'Whatever happened to saving?'. The answer came swiftly back. 'You killed it'.

If you are using credit in any of its forms, and most of us do, you need to look at the causes and consequences of indebtedness, and how people react when credit turns its darker face on your family.

Causes of Debt

There are three possible factors that might be working to get you into debt:

- changes for the worse in your income

- rises in short- or long-term costs

- over-commitment of your current income.

All these can lead to difficulty paying your present obligations, and we examine them in some detail below. If you are experiencing any of the following, you may be heading for a debt problem.

Loss of income
A reduction in income can occur in many ways:

* Loss of a job for yourself or another member of your household.

* A period of time away from work owing to accident, sickness or a strike.

* Fall in weekly or monthly pay owing to loss of over-time, short-time working, lay-offs, or other factors.

* If you are self-employed, reduction in earnings owing to lost commission or through a general reduction in business.

* Rise in income tax, leading to a reduction in take-home pay, owing to a change in circumstances (e.g. after separation or divorce).

* Loss or reduction in statutory benefits owing to changed circumstances. You may no longer be eligible for a particular benefit. Changes in government policy can affect entitlement.

* Loss of partner's earnings. Your family income may depend substantially on what your partner earns. If this ceases or is reduced, there is a problem, particularly if it is coupled with the additional expenditure that a new baby brings.

* Loss or reduction of part-time income of any sort.

* Reduction in income on retirement.

* Loss of financial help in cash or kind given by your employer, a relative or friend.

* Running out of savings which have been used to pay bills. This is different from the other losses of income, but just as important.

* When a relationship or marriage breaks down, the partner left caring for any children will often suffer financially, trying to pay for fixed overheads from a substantially reduced income.

A loss of income in itself may not be a catastrophe. Everything will depend on the extent of the loss and the level of commitment against your former income. Any loss of income should be accompanied by a look at current spending and at what is owed. Many people coping with the emotional traumas of unemployment fail to pay sufficient attention to the drastic loss of income that normally accompanies job loss. It often takes time to appreciate exactly how the drop in income will affect your spending power and, by the time adjustments start to be made, debts have frequently already been incurred. Income and expenditure need constant monitoring so that changes can be recognised and dealt with before they produce indebtedness.

Increase in expenditure
Unfortunately it is often the case that we gain extra commitments without a corresponding rise in income to meet them. This is due not to carelessness or bad budgeting, but to factors completely outside our control or that arise as a normal part of life. You and your partner may have a new baby and not have realised quite how much this would cost in both loss of income and increase in expenditure. Research into indebtedness shows that there is a very close relationship between the incidence of debt and families with young children. So, if you gain another long-term dependant, you could find it hard to meet the extra costs for a time. In addition, the following circumstances can produce an unexpected or higher than expected increase in expenditure:

* Moving, from rented to mortgaged property, from one location to another, into your own property for the first time, either rented or mortgaged. You may need to move as a result of getting married or taking the decision to live with somebody. You may need to move nearer to a new job. You may feel that you do not have enough room where you presently live, or that you want to make the move into owner-occupation, which is held out as being the best housing option. This is perfectly

reasonable, if you are not heavily committed with other costs already; but you may have failed to take everything into account and find yourself overstretched. If you have to move to a high-cost region (e.g. to London from the provinces) it may involve you in exceptional extra costs. If the move is accompanied by a loss of income at the time or later, difficulties may result.

* Having stretched yourself to become an owner-occupier, you may find that an increase in interest rates, producing a rise in your mortgage repayments and in other credit repayments, causes problems.

* You could have taken out a secured loan or second mortgage to make essential repairs or carry out home improvements. You may have borrowed to furnish or carpet your home. Many people underestimate the impact this sort of commitment can make on their overall budget.

* Essential services such as gas and electricity can cost more than you had allowed for. This could be due to inflation, a price rise, or a period of exceptionally cold weather. Telephone bills may be greater than usual owing to increased calls trying to obtain employment or calling a relative who is seriously ill.

* A sudden unexpected cost may arise, such as a funeral or a fine, and throw your budget out. Many people face occasional penalties for motoring offences. Others, having become guarantors for a friend's loan, can end up having to 'pay it off'.

* If you run a car, especially an older one, you will know the strain that keeping it in working order can place upon your budget.

* An uninsured loss, through fire or burglary, can cause unexpected capital expense in replacing lost items.

* You may need to find the money to repair or replace a household item such as a refrigerator or washing machine.

* You may need new glasses, dental treatment or some other essential health-related item.

* You may find yourself subsidising an unemployed son or daughter who lives with you.

* School expenses can be a problem. Uniform, school trips, holidays, photographs, music lessons, can all affect a tight budget, although it is always difficult not to pay for these items, which children regard as vitally important.

If any of these situations have arisen, it is worth asking yourself what they have cost and how that has affected your budget. Planning for unexpected expenditure is very difficult, but when it occurs action needs to be taken immediately.

Over-commitment
Everyone realises that over-commitment inevitably leads to debt, but deciding whether you are over-committed may be difficult. It is one thing to feel a general unease about whether you have enough money. This is probably a very good thing. It recognises the importance money plays in life and how the lack of it can badly affect you. It is, however, another thing to come to see you are actually in, or going to be in, trouble. There are some common early warnings of problems to come that should tell you to reappraise your circumstances:

* You are overdrawn at the bank at the end of every month. The bank manager often writes to you about it and you rely on a windfall or special payment to keep you going.

* The bank manager asks you at least twice a year not to use your cheque card or to pay by cheque.

* If you have no bank account there are one or two days a week or fortnight when you have no money at all. Some

weeks you may have to borrow a little from friends or relatives to tide you over.

* You have not been able to make all the payments you should on some of your credit payments. This means you may be getting letters, telephone calls or knocks at the door asking you to pay off the arrears.

* You have to postpone a new purchase you have looked forward to and believe you need, because you realise you do not have enough money.

* You postpone or cancel a holiday.

* You cannot send the children on a school holiday or outing they very much want to go on.

* You dread birthdays and Christmas because of the costs involved. You feel you cannot buy proper presents or food and drink.

* You find yourself borrowing money to pay off mortgage or rent arrears, fuel and other bills or just to maintain your standard of living.

Consequences of Indebtedness

Being unable to pay leads to worry. This raises questions about how you cope, or fail to cope, with that worry. Common responses are:

* Failure to open letters that you know are from creditors demanding money.

* Refusing to open the door to creditors who visit to collect payments.

* Ignoring the problem and hoping that it will go away.

* Arguments with your partner about who is to blame, involving accusations that the other has been irresponsible or a bad manager, or has failed to cope adequately.

These sorts of responses to financial worry are very negative. They either postpone the problem until it cannot be ignored because it has become so huge, or they threaten to destroy the basis of family relationships. If marital breakdown is a cause of debt, there is no doubt that indebtedness is a cause of marital breakdown. That is bad enough, but a recent NSPCC report recorded that the three stress factors most often reported to be affecting families where child abuse occurs are:

- marital discord

- unemployment

- debt

Debt is a persistent destructive and demoralising experience, eating away at the things we value most – our security, our self-respect, and our family relationships.

Steps in the Debt Experience

Having crossed the line from being a socially acceptable credit-user into being a debtor, there are well-documented stages of experience, which can be likened to steps down a staircase into financial despair:

DENIAL

REALISATION/SHOCK

GUILT–ANGER–AGGRESSION

SEARCH FOR A SOLUTION

HOPELESSNESS

LOSS OF HOUSE/GOODS/SERVICES

LOSS OF SELF RESPECT/PARTNER/FRIENDS/
CHILDREN

The object of this book is to take you off the staircase, at whatever stage you have reached, and put you on an escalator back towards self-help, self-respect, and, we hope, solvency.

One family's experience of debt

We have been dealing with statistics, causes, consequences, facts in abstract. Now is the time to examine the experience of debt of one family who came to the Birmingham Settlement Money Advice Centre when they had reached step 6 on the staircase, and were just about to lose their home. We shall call them Alan and Joan and they will tell us how they started on the staircase of debt and about their experience of descending into financial chaos.

THE START OF DEBT

Alan and Joan are a married couple in their mid-thirties, with three children aged 12, 5 and 3. Their experience of debt started when Alan lost his job as an electrician.

Alan – 'I had worked for the same company for ten years and felt I had to move to improve my position. I got this job eighteen months ago, which was more money and responsibility. We felt that the time had come to leave our rented housing association property and buy our own place. It was really now or never, and in any event the flat where we were living was getting too small with the family growing up. We found an older terraced type property which was in our price range and got a mortgage from a large national building society.

'To start with everything was great, the children had more space, and a garden to play in, and Joan and I felt that we had made a great step forward. Then the bombshell struck. I was made redundant, and because I'd only been at the firm a short while, I got no redundancy payment.

'I knew we'd have to go into debt because the unemployment benefit plus supplementary benefit just wasn't going to be enough to cover all our commitments, but I thought it would only be a temporary difficulty and as soon as I got back into work I'd be able to catch up on the payments I'd missed.

'I decided not to tell the building society and the other people that we owed money to that I had lost my job. I thought they'd lose confidence in me, and anyway it was a temporary thing while I got another job.'

DENIAL

Joan – 'It was a terrible shock when Alan lost his job – he'd been doing so well. To start with we were fairly cheerful, talking about what sort of job he should go for this time. But as the weeks went by, it became clear that getting another job was going to be hard. Alan became very depressed and I didn't like to worry him with money problems as well. I found myself paying the people who called at the door because it was difficult to say "no" to them, and so gas and electricity payments got further behind. I hid the bills from Alan hoping he would get another job soon and then we could pay.'

Alan – 'I was desperately trying to find work and by this time any job would do. The mortgage wasn't getting paid, and I had stopped opening letters from the building society because I knew there was nothing I could do. As the weeks turned into months, all our creditors were getting difficult and it got to the stage where we dreaded the post arriving or a knock on the door.'

REALISATION/SHOCK

Joan – 'Then this one week came, I'll never forget it. We'd had an official looking envelope through the post and shoved it behind the clock with all the others. On the Friday morning I was about to go shopping when there was a knock on the door. The electricity man had come to disconnect us. I couldn't believe it, that this could happen to us. He said to avoid disconnection I'd have to make an arrangement to pay straight away. I

agreed to pay £15 per week, and gave him £20 there and
then. It was the money I was going to spend on food.
When he'd gone I went into the back room and opened
all the letters. I discovered that we were in court on the
next Monday over the mortgage, that Alan hadn't been
paying it.'

GUILT—ANGER—AGGRESSION

Joan – 'I was furious with Alan – how could he have let
things drift and done nothing about the mortgage. I'd
given up so much to keep the children fed, I'd had to
cope with the electricity problem and I was going to try
and find the £15 per week to keep the electricity on.'

Alan – 'When I got back from the Job Centre, Joan was
still angry. She said we'd lose the house and what
would happen then. I felt guilty that I'd let the family
down. I said I'd go down to the building society and
sort something out. I got the bus into town, that cost me
40 pence, and went to the building society offices. I
asked to see the manager but was told he was busy, that
they'd make an appointment for next week. That was
no good because we were in court on the Monday. I
demanded to speak to someone now. I suppose I just
panicked, but I started shouting, and they threatened
to call the police. After that they wouldn't talk and said
they'd see me in court.'

Joan – 'That was a terrible weekend, I hadn't enough
money to buy proper food, and the children kept complaining about being hungry. I felt guilty that I hadn't
been a better manager. Alan was in a bad way – shouting at the children one minute, almost crying with
worry the next. I felt angry with him that we would lose
our home, that we'd worked so hard for.'

Alan – 'I went to court on the Monday. There were other
people in the same boat as us. Cases were being dealt
with every few minutes then my name was called out. I
was told to go up to the front of the court to listen. I was
nervous, I can't remember what the building society

said. I was standing there and the Judge said had I got anything to say. I just said I was unemployed and I was sorry. The Judge said he'd make something called a suspended order. I'd have to pay the mortgage plus something off the arrears. It came to £230 per month. He asked if I could pay and I said if I could get a job I'd pay. I went home and told Joan we could keep the house for the time being but we'd have to find this extra money.'

SEARCH FOR A SOLUTION

Alan – 'We didn't know where to turn. We thought about selling something, but by this time the car had gone, and we only had the house and furniture left. We thought of borrowing some more money, but who would lend to us when we were already before the court?'

Joan – 'I started to look around to see if I could find a job, but it was difficult with three children to see how I could manage. More money seemed to be going into keeping the electricity connected, and the next thing was the gas board threatening to disconnect. There just didn't seem to be any answer.'

HOPELESSNESS

Alan – 'A few more weeks went by and things got worse. We were rowing nearly all the time, everything we thought of didn't seem to work and on top of it all I just couldn't pay the £230 a month for the house. Looking for a job became a secondary factor to worrying about money.'

Joan – 'It was hopeless, and I was thinking about whether it would be better if we split up and I took the children with me to my mother's, I had had enough, I just couldn't take any more.'

LOSS OF HOME/GOODS/SERVICES

Alan – 'The next thing was a letter from the court saying

the building society wanted possession. This time I didn't even bother to go to court because I'd got no money to offer. They fixed a day for eviction in four weeks time.'

Joan – 'The man was coming to disconnect the gas, but it didn't really matter any more because we were going to lose the house anyway.'

It was at this point that Alan and Joan heard about the Money Advice Centre.

Joan – 'I was all for going but Alan was reluctant. He said they'd be do-gooding social workers who would just dish out sympathy. I said we must go, it was worth trying anything, and I was really glad we went, because it we hadn't we'd have been out on the streets, and I don't think our marriage would have survived.'

At the Money Advice Centre we analysed their income and outgoings. It was too late to save the house but after negotiation the building society were prepared to hold the eviction for twelve weeks to enable Alan and Joan to try and sell the property themselves.

We contacted a local housing association, explained the circumstances, and Alan and Joan were offered a ground-floor maisonnette with a garden.

Alan – 'By the time the house was sold and we'd paid all the costs including the court costs, there was nothing left for us. We'd only been in the house a short while and so it hadn't really had chance to appreciate in value. We still had other debts to the gas and electricity boards and for furniture we'd bought on hire purchase, a finance company loan and money owed on a credit card. The Money Advice Centre sorted all that out for us leaving us to concentrate on selling the house, and getting a job.'

LOSS OF SELF-RESPECT, PARTNER, FRIENDS, CHILDREN

Joan and Alan did not lose each other, although they came close to it, and they managed to keep their children and friends. But they lost their home, cannot afford items they previously took for granted, and have had to postpone a holiday to visit Alan's mother in Scotland. Even though Alan has now found work after twelve months on benefit, they will have a fearfully tight budget for some years to come while they try to clear their debts, rescheduled for them by the Money Advice Centre.

There are other losses, less easy to explain – loss of confidence in themselves and each other, and a loss of self-respect.

Alan – 'I always thought debtors were people who were dim or, if not, then were irresponsible – that it would never happen to someone like me. When it did, I felt angry, guilty, bewildered. I still feel that I've let myself and the family down, and wish we were still at the old house. I blame myself for what's happened, but I also feel angry about the job. If I hadn't been made redundant none of this would have happened, and I feel bitter about the level of benefits which we were expected to live on. We'd never been in debt before, I'd always paid my way. The creditors knew that I'd always paid in the past, but when we got into difficulty, that didn't stop them pursuing us for money which they knew we didn't have. I've lost self-respect and self-confidence, and I'm still worried about the future.'

Joan – 'I feel that we've been through all that for nothing – we're back to square one in rented accommodation again. It's had a bad effect on us all; the children have had to move schools and it's been hard explaining to them why we had to leave the house and move here where they haven't any friends. Before I always let Alan handle everything, but I've lost confidence in him a bit. Maybe that's a good thing because I'll ask more questions in the future and we'll think more carefully before we take on new commitments. I just wish we could have got more advice when things first started to go wrong, and we might still have the house.'

Alan and Joan and the children have all suffered, and are still deeply affected by a scarring experience. The hurt will pass, but the memory and the fear will remain, influencing future actions and affecting future aspirations.

Who Is to Blame for Debt?

One question Alan and Joan constantly raised during their experiences was their own sense of guilt for having let this happen to themselves. They were certainly to blame in some respects. For example:

* Alan never told the building society he was out of work or explained his problems to any of his creditors.

* Alan and Joan didn't talk to each other enough about their problem; both hoped it would just go away. Alan thought he'd get a job and be able to pay off the arrears. Joan just left it to Alan.

* Neither kept to the bargains they had made with creditors. They had good reasons for this, but told no one.

On the other hand, these are very human mistakes born out of anxiety. Alan felt if he told the building society he was out of work, they would not help him. Joan felt if she pressed Alan he would feel she did not trust him. They were confused and made a mistake, but understandably so.

There were factors at work in this case, however, that had nothing to do with them:

* Alan was made redundant because of the economic recession. This was not Alan's fault. He was out of work because his firm did not compete effectively in the engineering market long before Alan went there, and because the world recession has meant unemployment in general. Had he been able to get a job quickly, he would still have his own house.

* Alan and Joan could not acquire the sort of property they needed within the rented sector. This, coupled with government policy encouraging home-ownership, forced them to look at purchasing a home.

* Alan and Joan never had a high income, but the constant advertising of goods and credit on television and in the newspapers encouraged them to furnish much of their new home on credit, instead of waiting and making do with what they already had.

* For a while Joan paid the creditors who knocked on the door to the detriment of the more important ones who did not, but her failure to get her priorities right was partly as a result of the collection system in which she found herself.

* The wide availability of credit and the way in which payment is enforced were partly to blame for Joan and Alan's trouble. They were encouraged to borrow and they did. They had a misfortune and they ended up losers. They were victims of the consumer credit society as well as ignorant of what to do when in money trouble.

There will always be casualties in a society where credit is freely available. The problem is that there are not enough first aid stations, and the courts, where most of the casualties end up, are badly organised when attempting to deal with the modern problem of the individual consumer debtor. This is an argument not for restricting credit to certain categories of the community but for improving advice services and court proceedings for those who have the misfortune to become casualties.

The rest of this book sets out what can be done to help yourself, and suggests some proposals for change so that the Alans and Joans of the future have a better chance of dealing with the situation in which they find themselves.

2

Using Credit

When we purchase furniture, electrical items, clothes or a car, we spend some time deciding which make best suits our requirements. Price, preference, quality, after-sales service and appearance are compared, and the choice we make is based on our considered judgement of the options.

The same kind of thought and consideration ought also to go into looking for the right sort of credit with which to make our purchases. It usually does not. Many borrowers take the credit that is offered by the seller of the item they are purchasing, without considering other, maybe cheaper, sources of credit.

This chapter sets the different credit options available and what factors to take into consideration the next time you borrow.

What Is Credit?

Credit is simply lending money to make money. The lender charges the borrower for the use of his capital. The charge is called interest. Interest is shown as a percentage of the capital sum loaned, and it is then added on to the amount to be repaid.

The amount of interest a lender will charge will depend on many factors, the two main ones being:

● the risk the lender is taking, based on the borrower's ability to repay;

● the basic rate of interest set by the clearing banks.

Unfortunately, the lower your income, the less secure your job, the poorer you are, the higher will be the cost of any credit you will be able to get, since the lender will consider your ability to repay as high risk.

The lender will also need to take into consideration bank base rate. The main clearing banks fix a base (lowest) rate for lending. It is difficult to borrow money at a rate of interest lower than bank base rate, although some shops do offer low interest or interest-free credit to enable them to sell goods to purchasers who cannot pay cash. This can be a good deal, although it is sensible to check the price that you are paying for the goods 'interest free' with the price you would pay elsewhere for cash, which may be cheaper. In general, however, bank base rate sets the scene for credit charges. Recently it has fluctuated between 10 per cent and 14 per cent, but most individuals will be unable to borrow at base rate. Charges for borrowing from a bank or finance house will usually start at 4 per cent more than base rate.

To a credit-user the amount of interest that will be charged is *crucial*. The lower the interest then, generally speaking, the more advantageous to you is the credit. Working out the *real* rate of interest is however not so simple as it seems. There may be a flat rate of interest, but also other charges such as a documentation fee, administrative charges, or collection charges.

To help borrowers compare the costs of different forms of credit, the Consumer Credit Act 1974 introduced a uniform way of describing and calculating interest and other charges, which every lender must use. It is designed to show the *total* charge that you are paying for borrowing as a percentage, and is called the annual percentage rate or APR. The way the APR is actually calculated is very complex, but you do not need to understand the mathematical formula, you just need to know that the APR of any sort of borrowing gives you a yardstick by which to judge its cost.

Ways of Obtaining Credit

In order to 'shop around' for credit, a borrower needs to be aware of the various types of credit and credit-granters, and the differences between them.

The first differences to understand are those between:

- fixed-term and revolving credit,

- secured and unsecured credit.

Fixed-term credit v revolving credit
Fixed-term credit is where you know from the start how much and for how long you are borrowing and what it will cost in interest. For example:

> Ann Jones approaches her bank manager for a loan. She wishes to borrow £600. He explains that, spread over two years, the loan will cost £740.16 with monthly instalments of £30.84, or, if she spreads it over four years, it will cost more, namely £891.84, but with lower monthly instalments of £18.58.

The monthly instalments may fluctuate slightly when the bank base rate changes, but basically the costs and sums involved are clear.

With **revolving credit** or running-account credit, you are given credit, usually up to a maximum amount, *but* the amount borrowed fluctuates depending on what you buy or pay out or pay in. For example:

Ann Jones applies for an in-store credit card, with a borrowing ceiling set at £600. She can purchase goods in the store up to that value as and when she chooses and repay by monthly instalments that are adjusted according to what she owes.

Interest is charged on the outstanding balance at a rate that varies with the fluctuations in bank base rate. The credit agreement has no finishing point as with fixed-term credit and continues for as long as the borrower wishes to use the credit facility and owes money.

Secured v unsecured credit

Secured credit is where the credit-granter asks you to offer security for the loan. This is usually your house or an insurance policy. If you default on any one payment, the credit agreement normally provides for the credit-granter to call in the whole loan, and if that is not paid within a certain period of time (usually 28 days) the credit-granter is then entitled to go to court and ask for possession of your house. The house is then sold to pay off the debt.

Unsecured credit is where the lender relies on your receiving sufficient income in the future to repay the amount borrowed plus interest.

Credit-granters and types of credit

BANKS

The High Street banks offer many different credit facilities including:

* *Overdraft* – borrowing up to an amount agreed with the bank manager, normally on a current account. Interest is calculated daily on how much is outstanding. The interest rate is normally 4–6 per cent above bank base rate. Unapproved overdrafts can attract

higher rates of interest. An overdraft facility is generally considered to be the cheapest form of commercial borrowing. However, the bank has the right to withdraw the facility at any time unless specific agreement has been made to the contrary. In addition, any transactions on an overdrawn account are likely to be very expensive on bank charges. Security may also be required before an overdraft facility is granted.

* *Personal loan* – Cash loan, usually unsecured, for purchasing a specific item (e.g. a car). Repayment is usually by fixed regular payments over two to three years, with interest built in from the beginning. You can expect to pay 19–24 per cent APR.

* *All-purpose account* – called different things by different banks. Basically an account that pays you interest if you use it to save and charges you interest if you use it to borrow. When in debit the account operates as a revolving credit account, and interest is charged on the outstanding balance. You can expect to pay in the region of 25 per cent APR.

* *Mortgages.* The banks have now moved into the granting of first mortgages to owner-occupiers, an area that traditionally belonged to the building societies.

* *Home improvement loans* – Fixed-term secured credit at lowish rate of interest which attracts tax relief. Basically a second mortgage. In some banks, attracts an APR as low as 15 per cent.

In addition to the above, most High Street banks offer other forms of more specialised credit to individual customers, and many other financial services.

BANK CREDIT CARDS   (Access, Visa, Trustcard)
These bank credit cards entitle the holder to purchase goods and services from shops, restaurants, garages and other suppliers who have made an arrangement with the issuers of the cards. They are in effect a

revolving credit account, with a top limit fixed in each
case by the issuer of the card. Payment is by monthly
instalments – normally a minimum payment of 5 per
cent of what you owe each month. You can pay more. If
you settle the whole monthly bill in full you pay no
interest, thus getting 25–60 days' interest-free credit. If
not paid in full, interest is charged in the region of 27
per cent APR, varying with the bank base rate. Although the clearing banks own this credit facility, it is
not necessary to have a bank account to obtain a bank
credit card.

CREDIT IN SHOPS
Most of the High Street shops now offer credit facilities
to customers wishing to purchase goods. Customers
are encouraged to use the in-store credit facility since
research indicates that shoppers spend between two
and five times more in shops when using credit rather
than paying cash.

The forms of credit available in shops are usually:

* *Credit card charge account.* The customer is provided
with a credit card and a credit limit. Repayments are by
flexible monthly repayment. Interest is charged on the
outstanding balance. This is a revolving credit account.

* *Credit card budget account.* The customer is provided
with a credit card and a credit limit. Repayment is by
fixed monthly instalments to enable the borrower to
'budget' accurately.

* *Personal loan account.* The customer is offered a fixed-
term account with the interest built in from the beginning over a fixed repayment period – say two years.
Monthly instalments are fixed when the loan is entered
into.

* *Interest-free credit.* Instead of paying cash for the item,
you spread the cash price over several monthly instalments (usually 6–12 months).

Many stores are prepared to offer 'instant' credit to customers, which enables them to use the credit facility immediately to purchase goods. Most in-store credit is not financed by the shop, but by a bank or finance company to whom the borrower owes the money. APRs on shop credit vary from approximately 28 per cent to 40 per cent depending upon the sort of shop and how payment is to be made.

OTHER CREDIT CARDS

Other retail outlets, garages or discount warehouses also offer credit card facilities. These operate in the same way as shop credit and are nearly always financed by banks or finance companies and not by the retailers. APRs are likely to be 28–40 per cent.

CHARGE CARDS

Diners Club and American Express are *charge cards* as opposed to credit cards. The difference is that a monthly account is submitted by the card issuer that has to be paid in full each month. These cards offer an easy means to pay and a period of 20–40 days' interest-free credit, but it is easy to miss a payment and interest on default is high.

MAIL ORDER/CATALOGUE

Catalogue buying is a very popular way of purchasing clothing and other consumer goods. Catalogue companies have no retail outlet but distribute a glossy brochure to agents who act on their behalf. Payment is by fixed instalments collected weekly by the agent over 20–40 weeks. There is no extra interest charge for paying over a period except where stated, usually on large expensive items such as videos. Nevertheless, on comparing the cost of catalogue items with similar items on sale for cash in High Street shops, it was found that catalogue prices were 5–15 per cent higher, giving an equivalent average APR of up to 45 per cent. Catalogue buying thus has its price. If default occurs, a 'service charge' may be imposed, thus increasing the amount owed. Agents receive a commission on sales and must forward the payments that they collect to the catalogue company. Agents can be tempted to use instalments that they have collected to pay their own debts. *They must not do this*, since it can lead to criminal proceedings.

HIRE PURCHASE

This is a three-way credit transaction involving customer, retailer and financier. The customer chooses the goods he wishes to purchase, the retailer then sells them to a finance company (the owner), which *hires* them back to the customer, now known as the hirer, who pays the finance company by fixed monthly instalments. Interest is built in at the beginning of the agreement and is in the region of 34 per cent APR. The customer/hirer does not become the owner of the goods until the last instalment is paid with the option to purchase fee. In the meantime he can use the goods, but must take care of them, and cannot sell the goods since they belong to the owner/financier. If the hirer defaults on payment, the goods can be repossessed by the finance company and sold. When one-third of the hire purchase price has been paid by the hirer, the goods become 'protected goods' and the owner cannot repossess the goods without a court order.

CREDIT SALE AGREEMENT

This is a fixed-term agreement in writing to purchase specific goods by more than five instalments. Usually entered into on shop premises and frequently confused with hire purchase. On default, however, there is no right of repossession, and the creditor has to enforce the loan in the same way as any unsecured loan, by ultimately suing through the civil courts. Some fuel boards sell appliances on credit sale. Expect an APR in the region of 28–34 per cent.

CHECK OR VOUCHER TRADING

The credit-granter issues a check or voucher to the customer, which is exchangeable at shops that have a prior agreement with the check-trading company. The shop or shops are paid in full by the check trading company, which then collects fixed payments from the customer, including the interest that was fixed when the check was issued. Collections are usually made weekly by door-to-door collectors. You can expect to pay an APR of over 60 per cent on this sort of credit.

FINANCE COMPANIES

As a result of deregulation, finance companies have rapidly expanded their activities in the United Kingdom over the last fifteen years, and now compete with the banks to offer many financial services. The main credit facility they offer is the personal loan. This has traditionally been on a fixed-term basis, but increasingly loan accounts are being opened on a revolving credit basis. There is also a trend towards secured lending by finance companies, which allows them to offer lower rates of interest because they have a realisable asset to fall back upon if default in payment occurs. This makes lending less risky.

Secured lending attracts APRs of 19–24 per cent. Unsecured lending is likely to start at 26 per cent and averages 32 per cent. However, loans with APRs of over 100 per cent are not uncommon where the borrower is considered high risk, or small sums have been borrowed which are more expensive to service.

MONEYLENDERS

Moneylenders are the local equivalent of the finance company, offering cash loans, both secured and unsecured, usually on a fixed-term basis. The amount of interest is normally fixed at the start of the agreement, with repayment by weekly or monthly instalments. Collection of instalments is often door-to-door. Some smaller moneylenders will operate on a particular housing estate or in a suburb, and will have a small number of clients whom they know personally. This form of unsecured lending, often to those without bank accounts, is considered high risk, collection is labour intensive and therefore high rates of interest are usual, starting at 60 per cent APR and going as high as 1,000 per cent APR. (See the section on extortionate credit, p. 42.)

CREDIT BROKERS

A moneylender running his own loan business may also act as a credit broker for a larger finance company, arranging loans for and taking a commission from, the finance company.

TALLYMAN

The tallyman is a doorstep salesman offering clothes, bed-linen and other household items on credit with interest built in from the start. The tallyman collects small instalments weekly, normally over 13–26 weeks. For this form of credit APRs are unlikely to be less than 60 per cent and will frequently be over 100 per cent.

BUILDING SOCIETIES

In January 1987, as a result of legislative changes, the building societies hope to be able to broaden their financial services and move into insurance, estate agency, second mortgages and unsecured lending, thus enabling them to compete fully with banks and finance companies in the personal credit market.

Choosing the Right Type of Credit

Never be tempted to use credit on impulse without first carefully considering the implications of the type of credit on offer. You should always 'shop around' for credit and decide which suits your requirements best. You need to consider:

- the cost of the credit

- the length of time it will take to repay

- the repayments required

- the method of repayment

- the reputation of the credit-granter

- the consequences if you default

- the convenience of the credit

- whether you can afford the credit.

The cost of credit
The cost of credit (the amount that you are charged for having the use of the lender's money) can be measured in several ways:

* the flat rate of interest;

* the APR;

* the add-on cost (the total amount of the interest and other charges);

* the amount of the instalments.

In practice, the flat rate of interest tells you very little about the cost of credit and can be misleading when attempting to compare different types of credit. The APR is a better guide since it enables you to compare like with like. However, the other two factors are also very important, as can be seen in the following example:

Ann Jones wants to borrow £3,000 to buy a car. She approaches a bank where the manager tells her she can:

Plan A Borrow £3,000
Repayable over 18 months
at £195.74 per month
APR 23.1%
The loan plus interest plus other charges will cost a total of £3,523.32
The add-on cost is therefore **£523.32.**

OR

Plan B Borrow £3,000
Repayable over 90 months
at £75.67 per month
APR 23.1%
The loan plus interest plus other charges will cost a total of £6,810.30
The add-on cost is therefore **£3,810.30.**

She approaches another bank, which offers her:

Plan C Borrow £3,000
Repayable over 90 months
at £66.37 per month
APR 21.7%
The loan plus interest plus other charges will cost a total of £5,973.30
The add-on cost is therefore **£2,973.30.**

Which is the best deal? If Ann can afford repayments as high as £195.74 per month, Plan A is the best deal for her. If she wishes to reduce her monthly payments by spreading the loan over a much longer period of time, Plan C is better than Plan B because its monthly repayments are smaller over the same period of time.

We have seen how bank base rate and credit-worth-iness can affect the cost of credit, but there are other factors that credit-granters take into account:

* Whether the loan is secured or unsecured. Finance companies will maintain that by accepting security for a loan, they are able to reduce the interest rate because the loan is less risky. In practice this is not always the case and it is sometimes possible to obtain an un-secured loan from a bank at a more advantageous cost.

* The cost to the credit-granter of administering the loan. Both the documentation fee and the cost of collection can affect the cost of credit. Administrative costs on a loan of £100 are often as great as on a loan of £3,000, but £30 costs added on to a loan of £100 create an astro-nomical APR, whereas added on to a loan of £3,000 they do not.

   If the lender offers the borrower the facility of door-to-door collection, the cost of the collector's time will be reflected in the total cost of the credit, as in the follow-ing example:

Angela Evans wants to borrow £100. She ap-proaches a local moneylender who offers:

Borrow £100
Repayable over 28 weeks
   at £4.85 per week
APR 220%
The loan plus interest plus charges will cost a total
   of £136.00
The add-on cost is therefore **£36.00.**

These figures seem small, but in the context of a loan over only 28 weeks, Angela Evans is paying £36.00 for the use of the £100, and an APR of 220%. The reasons for this are partly that the moneylender will consider her a high risk, partly that he collects door-to-door, and partly that he wants to make a substantial profit.

The repayment term

The repayment term, or length of time the loan will take to pay back, is an important consideration. It often looks advantageous to spread a loan over a longer period of time because it reduces the instalments, but it also increases the add-on cost, as we have already seen.

More importantly, borrowing over an extended period of time can increase the risk of something going wrong. We may be able to predict over a period of 12 months that our job is secure and what our expenditure on other items is likely to be, but to predict over five years is far more difficult, and thus far more risky.

The repayments required

You need to consider the amount of the instalments and how this will fit into your future budget, and whether repayments are weekly or monthly. If you are on a tight budget, weekly repayments are likely to be easier to manage than monthly. On the other hand, weekly credit is generally more expensive.

When looking at repayments you must decide between opting for fixed-term credit, where you know exactly what your monthly or weekly payment will be, and for which you can therefore budget, or revolving credit, where your monthly repayments will depend on how much you have spent in the previous account period. If you decide to use revolving credit, you should always try to repay more than the 'minimum repayment figure' otherwise you can get trapped into an infinite repayment schedule.

Alan Smith applies for a bank credit card. He needs credit to furnish his new house and decides to use it also for purchasing petrol, clothing and car repairs. He is given a credit limit of £600. His account runs like this to start with:

Date	Balance brought forward	Interest	Purchases	Balance	Minimum payment
Feb.	—	—	Furniture – £440 Petrol – £42 Car repairs – £108	£590.00	£29.50
Mar.	£560.50	£12.33	Clothing – £60 Petrol – £44	£676.83	£33.80
April	£643.03	£14.21	Petrol – £38 Other – £24	£719.24	£35.95

Alan finds he cannot afford to pay more than his minimum monthly payment, and needs to use the card to carry on making purchases. He has now exceeded his £600 limit. The credit card company write to him and extend his credit limit to £800. He continues to use the card and his account proceeds as follows:

Date	Balance brought forward	Interest	Purchases	Balance	Minimum payment
May	£638.29	£15.03	Petrol – £41 Household items – £18	£757.32	£37.85
June	£719.45	£15.82	Petrol – £36 Car repairs – £62	£833.27	£41.65
July	£791.62	£17.41	Petrol – £36 Holiday deposit – £80 Clothing – £8	£933.03	£46.65
Aug.	£903.33	£19.87	Petrol – £42 Household items – £16	£981.20	£49.05

By now Alan has exceeded his limit once more, his monthly minimum payments have risen in eight months from £29.50 per month to £49.05. Only by ceasing to use the card altogether can he hope to reduce his indebtedness, and pay less interest.

The method of repayment

This can be important with some forms of in-store revolving credit accounts. If you elect to pay your monthly payments by bankers' standing order, the credit can cost considerably less than if you pay by cash with a payment book. One store charges an APR of 28 per cent for standing order repayment and 36 per cent for cash repayment, presumably because it considers standing order payment more reliable.

You may find it convenient to have door-to-door collection rather than having to remember to make a regular payment. This will cost more, reflected in the APR that you pay.

The reputation of the credit-granter

It is *essential* that you only borrow from someone who has a licence to grant credit, issued by the Office of Fair Trading. Anyone advancing credit of more than £50 must be licensed. Under the Consumer Credit Act 1974, a licence will only be granted to a 'fit person', and trading without a licence is a criminal offence. If you find that you already have a loan with an unlicensed credit-granter, the Consumer Credit Act 1974 states that the loan cannot be enforced against you unless the Office of Fair Trading gives permission. In practice this usually means that the credit-granter cannot legally insist on you repaying the loan. If a licensed credit-granter behaves illegally or improperly, the Office of Fair Trading has the power to revoke the licence to trade.

Assuming the credit-granter has a licence, you still need to satisfy yourself that he/she is 'responsible'. If you or a friend or relative have borrowed in the past from a particular lender, completed the loan and found the lender satisfactory, that can be a guideline.

Broadly speaking the American-based finance companies tend to advertise, sell and market their credit fairly aggressively. It has been our experience that they also collect aggressively, and are unlikely to tolerate late payments or agree to reduced payments during times of financial difficulty.

Another thing to be extremely careful about is 'third-party' selling of credit. A reputable finance company is likely to want to satisfy itself that you can actually afford the repayments on the loan, but a third party advancing the credit may not care and may actually mislead you about the details of the agreement in order to sell you their goods. A double-glazing salesman is anxious to sell his product and if you cannot afford cash he may offer to arrange credit to 'help you' purchase his product. A salesman in a shop may be more anxious to collect his commission on both the sale of the goods and the sale of the credit to go with it than to ensure that you understand the precise details of the agreement, and whether you can afford the repayments. Many of the 'consolidated loan' advertisements that appear in local newspapers are inserted by credit brokers, who are anxious to sell finance and collect their commission for introducing the customer to a particular finance company. Be very careful in these sort of situations; a third party will usually put his own interests first and yours second. Whenever possible deal directly with the finance company involved. If that is not possible, see if another company will give you credit direct.

The consequences if default occurs
Borrowers seldom consider this aspect when entering into agreements, but it is particularly relevant when considering secured as against unsecured lending. The result of default in secured lending can be loss of home; with unsecured lending the creditor's remedy is to sue for the sum through the courts.

Always read the section of the agreement that deals with what will happen in the event of default, since some agreements charge interest on arrears. A revolving credit account is normally more expensive when default occurs, with interest being charged upon interest.

Always consider insurance (see below, p. 39) against sickness, accident, death and, if possible, unemployment, to protect your repayments in the event of default as a result of one of these occurrences.

Convenience

This factor appears to influence the majority of borrowers. It may be more convenient to borrow from a credit-granter who is already known to the borrower or available in the shop, but it might not be the best way of borrowing. Many people do not have bank accounts and are thus reluctant to approach banks for credit, assuming that they lend only to the middle or professional classes. This is largely no longer the case, and sometimes a bank loan can be cheaper than an in-store credit card. If you have not used a bank before it is worth considering for the future.

Catalogues are an extremely convenient method of purchasing, particularly if getting to the shops is expensive or a problem – for example, if you are disabled, elderly, have long working hours, or young children to care for. Sometimes convenience may outweigh other factors, such as cost.

Can you afford it?

When buying an item for cash we have to consider whether we can afford it. The same should apply with credit. This becomes particularly important when considering borrowing money from one lender to pay off several other existing debts. If you could not afford the original repayments, will you be able to afford the new repayment, and delay other purchases until you have paid off the new loan?

When embarking on credit you are well advised to take *all* these factors into account. Shopping around for credit may be tiresome and time-consuming, but it is usually worth a little time and effort to ensure you have made the right choice.

Who Gets the Credit?

The simple answer to this question is everyone. Credit is now more widely available than ever before, although some people will have to pay so much for credit that it may effectively bar them. The general rule is that the wealthier and more credit-worthy you are, the less you will pay to borrow money; the poorer you are, the more difficult it will be for you to find someone reputable to lend to you, and the more it will cost you because you are a 'risky' prospect.

Credit-granters have different ways of assessing prospective borrowers, which can roughly be sub-divided into:

- the objective approach – credit-scoring and credit-reference agencies

- the subjective approach – personal interview, or experience of the family or neighbourhood where the prospective borrower lives.

Whichever approach is used the borrower will usually be asked to fill in some sort of questionnaire about income, outgoings, other loans, etc. It is on this information that the credit-granter will largely rely. It is important that you give entirely accurate answers to the questions. If you deliberately lie to obtain credit you may be prosecuted for obtaining money or credit by deception.

Credit-scoring
An individual credit-granter runs a statistical check to discover which applicants are good payers and which are bad payers. Each factor dictating good or bad is then evaluated and given a 'score' on a questionnaire. Potential borrowers are asked to fill in the questionnaire and are scored to evaluate their probable payment performance. An owner-occupier in a professional job for ten years, married with one child and having a bank

account would score much higher than a divorced, un-skilled man living in rented accommodation who had held his present job for only six months. The credit-granter can fix a 'pass' and 'fail' mark, and usually will have an intermediate area that will be looked at again.

Credit-scoring is now becoming fairly sophisticated with the increasing computerisation available to the larger financial institutions, but it does fail to take account of personal differences.

If you have applied for credit and been rejected by one company, do not assume that you will be rejected by others. Each credit-granter will have a different system of scoring.

Credit-reference agency

Another important check a credit-granter can make is with a credit-reference agency to see if a potential borrower has been a bad payer in the past. These agencies deal with several million enquiries every year. They keep records of people who have been sued through the courts to judgement, and of bankruptcies. In some cases they may also keep additional information about occupation and enquiries made by other credit-granters about a particular borrower.

If you have been refused credit because of a credit-reference agency report you are entitled under the Consumer Credit Act 1974 to know the name and address of the agency and on request the agency must send you the information held on record about you. If the information is incorrect you can insist it is corrected. Any dispute will be settled by the Office of Fair Trading.

Personal experience/interview

Some credit-granters will come and interview you in your home and use the opportunity to arrive at an assessment of you as a good or bad payer in addition to asking you to fill in a form. This is increasingly rare, particularly with a great deal of credit business being conducted through the post.

Personal experience is most important for the local

moneylender or the door-to-door tallyman. He will often have long experience and good local knowledge and may have dealt with families over several generations. Typically a small loan will be advanced and if that is paid satisfactorily he will be prepared to lend again. However, beware of the door-to-door creditor who invites you to take advantage of a 'top-up loan'. In the following example you can see how disadvantageous this can be:

Hilary Reynolds borrows £30 from a moneylender. The total cost of interest, etc., is £2.97, making a total debt of £32.97 repayable over 21 weekly instalments of £1.57 at an APR of 52.2%.

Hilary pays for 12 weeks, so there is £14.13 left to pay. The moneylender offers her a further loan of £30. He gives her £30 less the £14.13 she still owes him, so she actually receives £15.87 in cash from the moneylender. She now has to repay a further £32.97 by 21 weekly instalments, but because nearly half of the new loan incorporates money outstanding on the old loan, she is paying interest twice over on part of the second loan, and a total APR of 63.6% on the second loan.

Red-lining
This is where a creditor or reference agency draws an imaginary red line around a whole area and effectively blacklists anyone who lives in that area, refusing to grant credit merely on the basis that the potential borrower lives in the 'wrong area'.

In theory this should not happen and each applicant for credit should be treated on his or her own merits. In practice it does happen, leaving the people in the area with no reputable source of credit and having to rely on backstreet moneylenders and loan sharks.

Insurance

It is possible to take out insurance with most bank and finance company loans, with most in-store credit, and with bank credit cards. When looking at insurance:

* Examine exactly what eventualities are covered. Some insurance covers only for accident, sickness and redundancy, while others give additional protection against unemployment.

* Look at the length of time for which the cover lasts. Some insurance will cover your repayments for only six months, others for 12 months, some for two years. Some creditors offer free automatic insurance, which may make their APR look more expensive than companies that quote insurance cover as an extra cost.

* When filling in the questionnaire, do not be put off by a salesman in a hurry. Make sure you answer all the questions accurately. Always give full details of any previous illness or injury, otherwise you may find the insurance company refusing to pay on the grounds that you failed to disclose a material fact. **Do take out insurance if it is available.**

Consumer Credit Protection

The Consumer Credit Act 1974 controls the way in which credit is granted in the UK, and gives certain protection and rights to the borrower. The Act contains 192 sections and is a very complex piece of legislation. We cannot do more than briefly summarise the major points of importance.

* The Act provides for the Office of Fair Trading with a Director General of Fair Trading to police the Act. The Office of Fair Trading is responsible for licensing credit-granters (and others) under the Act, and revoking licences where appropriate.

* The Act sets rules for the advertising of credit and for the canvassing of customers.

* The form and content of credit agreements is now subject to statutory control.

* The doctrine of 'cancellability' is introduced to some agreements.

* Creditors have statutory duties to give certain information to borrowers.

* The Act sets out rights to a rebate for early settlement, and other rights on termination of a regulated agreement.

* The Act seeks to control interest levels by introducing the concept of 'extortionate credit'.

* Finally, the Act introduces new regulations on default and 'time orders', which are dealt with in Chapters 8 and 9.

Some of the points have been covered in this chapter already, but there are also important facts at the point of entry into an agreement regulated by the Act, and thereafter. The majority of consumer credit agreements entered into by readers (i.e. those under £15,000) will be regulated by the Act.

The agreement
The Act carefully controls the contents of the agreement that you sign with the creditor. The statutory contents vary with the form of credit being dealt with, but broadly speaking the agreement must contain:

- Name and address of creditor
- Name and address of debtor

} all agreements

- Description of goods ⎫
  ───────────────────── ⎬ hire purchase, credit sale and
- Cash price of goods ⎭ conditional sale agreements

- Details of advance payments – all agreements where advance payments made

- Credit limit ⎫
  ───────── ⎪
- Rate of interest ⎬ revolving credit agreement
  ───────── ⎪
- Other charges ⎭

- Amount of credit ⎫
  ───────────── ⎪
- Total charge for credit ⎬ fixed-term agreements
  ───────────── ⎪
- Total amount payable ⎭

- Timing of repayments ⎫
  ────────────────── ⎪
- Amounts of repayments ⎬ all agreements
  ────────────────── ⎪
- APR (annual percentage rate) ⎭

- Variability of interest rate – all agreements where interest rate is variable.

- Details of security given – all agreements where security given (i.e. secured loans)

- Charges on default – all agreements where there are charges on default

The agreement must also have a section about your rights. If it is a cancellable agreement, it must inform you of your rights to cancel the agreement – you are entitled to a 'cooling-off period' and subsequent copies of the agreement to sign, or to give notice to cancel the agreement. Cancellable agreements are broadly those where the borrower has been the subject of 'face-to-face' persuasion, includes 'doorstep sales', and some selling of credit on trade premises, where the borrower takes the credit agreement away to sign.

Extortionate credit

The Act confers the right on a borrower to challenge the rate of interest chargeable under an agreement, even after the borrower has signed the agreement. The borrower will have to go to court and satisfy the judge that the rate of interest is grossly extortionate. Each case is decided upon its own facts, having regard to:

* prevailing interest rates at the time the agreement was entered into;

* age, experience, health and business capacity of the consumer;

* the degree and nature of financial pressure on the consumer when he entered into the agreement;

* the degree of risk accepted by the creditor, having regard to any security provided;

* the creditor's relationship to the consumer;

* whether or not the creditor quoted an accurate cash price for the goods or services;

* any other relevant factors.

If the court finds that there has been an extortionate credit bargain, it can re-open the whole agreement.

If you feel you have entered into an agreement with an extortionate rate of interest, it is advisable to seek legal advice before starting court proceedings, and to enquire about the availability of legal aid.

Rebate for early settlement

The Consumer Credit Act gives borrowers a statutory

right to complete payments ahead of the time set out in the agreement, and to receive a rebate of a proportion of the total credit charges for early settlement. If you wish to repay early you should ask your credit-granter for a settlement figure and he must provide it.

Duty to give information

The Consumer Credit Act imposes duties on creditors to provide debtors with information during the course of a credit agreement. Information on revolving credit agreements must be given periodically to the borrower even if he does not ask for it. The Act also imposes a duty on a creditor to provide a copy of the credit agreement and information on the state of the account when requested by the debtor in writing, and on payment of a small fee (50p).

Loan Sharks

We hope that you will never come into contact with a 'loan shark'. The general impression of a loan shark is a man in a smart overcoat and a large motorcar, cruising around a down-market area lending money at huge rates of interest and then enforcing repayment by threats of violence or by putting a brick through a window, or worse. People like this do exist. They are usually unlicensed moneylenders and are law-breakers. They should be reported to the Trading Standards Department of your local authority as soon as possible. If you are frightened to make a formal complaint by giving your name, it is still worthwhile making an anonymous complaint if it persuades the Trading Standards Officer to investigate.

Loan sharks can, however, also appear to be nice and friendly, charge high rates of interest and take away benefit books to ensure their repayments. This is illegal.

Do not hand over a benefit book to a creditor – seek advice from your money advice centre, Citizens' Advice Bureau, or Consumer Advice Centre.

Large companies that have an air of respectability may also be loan sharks, harassing borrowers for repayment in various ways. Harassment is against the law, so beware of these tactics and report them to the Trading Standards Department (see Chapter 3).

Miscellaneous Points on Using Credit

Guaranteeing a credit agreement
When credit companies are advancing credit to a younger person or to someone whom they regard as a high-risk borrower, they may ask the borrower to provide a guarantor. Guaranteeing a loan is a very serious business. It is not just witnessing the agreement, or vouching for the honesty of the borrower, who may be your work-mate, friend, neighbour or relative. *It is promising to pay the money if he or she does not.* Do not agree to guarantee a loan unless you are prepared to end up paying.

If you find yourself in the unfortunate position of having already guaranteed the loan of a defaulter, you may be sued by the credit company for the unpaid balance. Although you have to pay, you may in turn sue the person who has defaulted and try and recover some of the money back from him/her. Before doing this it is advisable to take some legal advice. It may be pointless if the person cannot pay.

Joint liability for credit/debts
Married couples or co-habitees often enter credit agreements jointly; in effect they both borrow the money. The law states that they become 'jointly and severally liable' for the repayments. This *does not* mean that each person owes half the debt. Both are liable to pay the whole debt. The company can elect whether to pursue one or both of them if default occurs. If one partner disappears the other partner must carry on making the total repayment and not half of it. Whilst people remain together, joint liability is not a problem, but it starts to

become important on separation or divorce. If one partner disappears leaving the other at the home address with the children, maybe with little or no income, this will not stop the finance company pursuing the partner whose whereabouts they know. Do not enter into a joint agreement unless you are prepared to accept these consequences in the event of the worst happening.

Death of a borrower

Broadly speaking, when you die your debts die with you. However, if a borrower dies leaving assets that legally form part of the deceased's estate, any debts must be paid from the estate by the administrator or executor.

If the debt is in the joint names of the deceased and another person who is living, then the lender can enforce the debt against the estate of the deceased *or* against the living party, since they are jointly and severally liable.

Where a borrower dies leaving no assets, the debt cannot be enforced against his or her nearest relative. A widow is *not* responsible for her deceased husband's debts and a widower is *not* responsible for his deceased wife's debts, unless they had signed the agreement jointly.

Credit Unions

The idea of a credit union – a sort of self-help saving and borrowing co-operative – is to provide a cheap source of credit for lower-income families or individuals.

Credit unions are run democratically and controlled by the members, who normally have some common bond through where they work, live or worship. Members join by paying an initial fee, and then saving regularly with the union. Each union is operated by a committee elected annually by its members to run the day-to-day affairs of the Union. A separate loans committee considers each application for a loan on its merits. The committee can make loans to members up to the amount saved by other members in any one week or month. Loans are usually small and interest is charged at less than 13 per cent APR. Repayment arrangements can be designed to suit the requirements of a particular member. Credit unions provide a highly advantageous cheap form of credit for their members. They are much cheaper than moneylenders, tallymen and catalogues, and can be thoroughly recommended.

The credit union movement has not expanded in England and Wales very quickly, but there are about 50 unions presently, and the numbers are growing. In Northern Ireland, where they tend to focus on the churches, there are approximately 100 unions with over 80,000 members. They are also popular in Eire, Scotland, Canada and the USA. In America, unions finance 15 per cent of consumer credit through 23,000 unions with 34 million members.

If you would like to join a credit union or start one in your area, information on where established unions exist and how to start one yourself can be obtained from:

> The Association of British Credit Unions Ltd
> P.O. Box 135
> Credit Union Centre
> High Street
> Skelmersdale
> Lancashire WN8 8AP

Conclusion

In conclusion we would like to propose the following basic rules you should follow when obtaining credit.

☞ *Do not borrow on impulse.* Think about it first, and shop around for the best deal. The financing of what you wish to buy is as important a choice as the choice of the particular goods or service itself.

☞ *Do not sign an agreement until you have read it carefully* and know what the borrowing will cost you and what can happen if you default.

☞ Do not sign an agreement unless you are confident that your lender is a reputable company or individual with a licence from the Office of Fair Trading.

☞ As a general principle, *always be careful, vigilant and suspicious*. When people borrow money they can sometimes feel unable to challenge or question the lender. This feeling is much stronger about borrowing money than it is about buying goods. It should not be, money is traded as a commodity and you are the lender's customer, just as you are the store's customer when purchasing a dining room suite. Do not buy your credit unless you feel you have the best deal available.

☞ *Insure your loan where possible.*

☞ *Make sure, before you buy your credit, that you can really afford the repayments.*

The credit society is here to stay. If we all ceased to borrow, manufacturing industry would be severely hit and trade would diminish. Our society needs the borrower as much as the lender. Borrowers should have the confidence to feel more equal in their credit shopping.

3

The Creditor's Experience of Debt

To a creditor who makes money by lending money, a defaulter or debtor seems a serious threat, striking at the heart of the profitability of the credit-granting company. If borrowers default in sufficient numbers the creditor would cease to have a viable business. In practice this hardly ever happens, but creditors are always fearful that it might, and treat debtors accordingly. The attitudes of creditors are thus rather too much rooted in the social values of a hundred years ago when civil debt was an offence punishable with imprisonment. An indication of this is found in their use of the term 'delinquency' to mean default.

Creditors argue that default is not only a serious threat to profits, but also reduces their ability to offer competitive rates of interest and has a knock-on effect, increasing interest rates for the other borrowers who do not default. In addition, default takes up much staff time and is thus expensive administratively. Although creditors often say debt enforcement is not cost effective, many tend to act quickly and severely with defaulters, since it is argued that were creditors to 'go easy' on defaulters this would open the flood gates to defaulting on a massive scale.

Even when default has occurred through no fault of the borrower, creditors believe that they are 'the injured party'. These attitudes mean that borrowers need to examine the creditor's rights on default in case they need to protect themselves.

The Creditor's Rights when Default Occurs

The rights of the creditor are largely controlled by the terms of the agreement or contract that the borrower has signed. Some agreements need to be within the conditions imposed by the Consumer Credit Act 1974, so a knowledge of that Act as it affects creditors is also needed.

Most agreements set out the creditor's right to terminate an agreement when default occurs, and additionally often give the right to start charging interest on arrears, known as **default interest**. The Consumer Credit Act restricts the amount of interest that can be charged as default interest to the original rate of interest under the agreement. So, if the interest rate chargeable under the agreement is 2.5 per cent per month, the agreement cannot provide for interest on default at a higher rate.

Under the Consumer Credit Act, if a customer is in default on even a single payment (or in breach of any other condition of the agreement), the creditor must give the borrower at least seven days' notice before he is entitled to

- terminate the agreement

- demand earlier payment

- recover possession of land or goods

- enforce any security

by sending a **default notice** to the borrower. The notice (amongst other things) must state:

* details of the alleged breach;

* what the borrower can do to remedy the breach (e.g. pay off the arrears);

* what the creditor will do if the breach is not remedied (e.g. terminate the agreement);

* the rights the borrower has to apply to the court for further time to pay (a time order – see Chapter 9);

* where the borrower might go to get advice.

In the case of a hire purchase agreement, different considerations apply because the creditor has the additional right to repossess the goods if the borrower defaults. However, where one-third of the hire purchase price has been paid by the borrower, the goods cannot be repossessed unless the creditor goes to court and the court orders repossession. Whether one-third has been paid or not, the creditor cannot enter the borrower's home or other premises belonging to the borrower to repossess the goods unless the borrower consents or the creditor gets an order from the court to do so.

When the creditor terminates the hire purchase agreement because of the borrower's default, what happens next is largely governed by the terms of the hire purchase agreement that the parties signed. The creditor normally sells the goods and then a calculation takes place to assess how much the borrower still has to pay, as in the following example:

Ray Woodward purchases a car on hire purchase. The actual cost of the car is £2,200. The hire purchase price (cost plus interest) is £3,300, payable in monthly instalments of £137.50. Ray pays for five months (£137.50 × 5 = £687.50) and then finds he cannot manage the repayments. He defaults and the creditor terminates the agreement and eventually repossesses the car. The car is sold at auction for £1,200. The creditor then claims the following from Ray:

2 months' arrears under the agreement		275.00
Plus the hire purchase price	3,300.00	
Less the arrears	275.00	
Less the option to purchase fee	5.00	
Less the payments made	687.50	
Less the sale price	1,200.00	
		1,132.50
TOTAL		£1,407.50

The creditor can sue Ray through the courts for £1,407.50 if he does not pay.

However, if Ray decides to terminate the agreement *before* the creditor terminates for his default, as he has the right to do in the case of a hire purchase agreement, a different set of calculations apply:

Ray decides he does not want the car any more because he is losing his job in the near future. He terminates the agreement and the hire purchase company repossesses the car. It is entitled to a 50% minimum payment under the Consumer Credit Act 1974 (re-enacting the Hire Purchase Act 1965), calculated as follows:

Hire purchase price =		3,300.00
Less 50%	1,650.00	
Less instalments paid	687.50	
		2,337.50
		£962.50

However, if the creditor can show that Ray did not take reasonable care of the car, it can also charge him for putting the car back into good order. For example, if the car has a dented wing the creditor can charge Ray for putting it right, at, say, the estimated price of £150. So Ray has to pay

$$
\begin{array}{r}
962.50 \\
+150.00 \\
\hline
£1,112.50 \\
\hline
\end{array}
$$

considerably less than if the creditor had terminated the agreement due to his default.

In addition, if Ray can show that the actual loss sustained by the creditor is less than £1,112.50, he will be liable to repay only the actual loss incurred by the creditor.

These complicated calculations arise because the goods belong to the creditor during the hiring period, and therefore the borrower is 'hiring' them, rather than in the case of most credit agreements, where the borrower owns the goods that he purchases with the credit advanced to him.

☞ **Important!**

If you have a hire purchase agreement that you wish to terminate or where you cannot manage the repayments, the wisest course is to seek advice *immediately* from a money advice centre, law centre, Citizens' Advice Bureau, or a legal aid solicitor.

Once an agreement (other than hire purchase) has been terminated, the creditor's actions are no longer controlled by the Act (except concerning the provisions for rebates for early settlement – see Chapter 2, p. 42). The creditor will then consider what action to take as a next step to recover his money.

Creditor's Steps after Default

The action that a particular creditor takes if default

continues unremedied will vary depending on the form of credit involved and the type of creditor. Different companies use different techniques, which can be summarised as follows:

- Head office – computerised letter technique

- Branch office – letter – telephone – visit technique

- Door-to-door collector – visit

- Instructing a solicitor to recover the debt (via the courts if necessary)

- Passing the debt on to a debt collector

- Selling the debt to a debt collector

- Taking court proceedings.

Head office – computerised letter
Large finance companies often deal with arrears cases from head office, particularly those that have no network of branch offices such as bank credit cards, shop credit cards, hire purchase companies and second mortgage companies. They use highly sophisticated computerised systems to manage arrears.

The computer is programmed to send out a series of letters, which will continue until either the defaulter pays, the series is finished, or an alternative arrangement is made concerning the arrears. A series of letters may look something like this.

Time after first missed payment	Letter No.	Type of letter
2 weeks	1	Gentle reminder
4 weeks	2	Stronger reminder (default notice under

		Consumer Credit Act 1974)
5 weeks	3	14 days to clear arrears
7 weeks	4	7 days to clear or we refer to solicitors/debt collector/ start court proceedings
8 weeks	5	We are referring case to solicitors

If the borrower contacts the company to explain why payments have not been made, or to ask for further time to pay, it is frequently the case that the computer does not get told and the letters keep on coming. It is important to keep on at the company to halt the computerised procedure once an agreement has been reached for reduced payments or further time to pay.

The disadvantages of this collection technique are that contacting head office can be a problem, long-distance telephone calls are costly, and letters are sometimes difficult to write. If letters are written and are ignored or lost at head office, this increases the borrower's feeling of isolation. The computer often seems too powerful, which is bad for the borrower who is going to have great difficulty in explaining to a machine the individual personal circumstances in which he finds himself.

Of course many head offices have staff who deal with debtors and whose personal case you become. In these cases the debt collection relationships are similar to those described in the next section.

Branch office – letters, telephone calls, visits
Creditors that have a branch office – banks, building societies, some national (and most local) finance companies – may use the branch office to pursue the debt.

From the creditor's point of view there are three advantages in this:

* the branch lent the money in the first place and should be responsible for collecting it;

* the branch office should know the borrower and his circumstances;

* the branch office is near to the borrower and the action that can be taken is wider – not only letters, but visits and telephone calls, can be used.

From the borrower's point of view, branch office collection can sometimes have disadvantages. The Birmingham Settlement Money Advice Centre has seen cases of branches harassing borrowers for repayment by persistent visits and telephone calls to home and work. This may be because pressure from head office can often be unfairly exerted on branch managers, who may fear that they are seen to be performing inadequately. The branch manager of a large American finance company held the following conversation with a money advice case worker:

Manager:	Your client must pay.
Case worker:	He can't, he's just lost his job and his income has been reduced by 60%.
Manager:	Can't he pay £5 per week?
Case worker:	If he pays you £5 per week his rent or electricity will suffer.
Manager:	He paid £10 last week.
Case worker:	That's because you kept pestering him and his wife couldn't take any more.
Manager:	It's all very well for you, I've got head office on to me saying – You lent the so and so money, you'd better get out there and collect it. Your figures are looking really bad compared with the other branches.
Case worker:	I'm sorry.
Manager:	My job's on the line.

The pressure from head office to collect the uncollectable is often passed on from the branch manager to the client.

On the other hand, branch office collection can be advantageous to the borrower, since it gives him the opportunity to visit the branch and discuss at some length his position with the branch employees, and possibly make an arrangement. No discussion is possible with a head office computer. On the other hand, a computer cannot feel afraid for his job!

Door-to-door collection

A local moneylender, tallyman or catalogue agent who collects weekly from the borrower is usually the first creditor to know if something is going wrong. When the caller arrives on a Friday and is told that there is no money to pay, he does not wait two weeks and then send a letter; he can and does ask questions there and then. The more reputable door-to-door collectors will accept the odd week missed, or even agree to accept reduced payments for a while until things improve financially. The less reputable will insist on payment, and it is very dificult to say 'I'm sorry, I cannot pay' to an aggressive collector who will not go away unless he is paid. It is particularly difficult if the neighbours are listening or watching and the collector insists on conducting the negotiations on the doorstep. Some moneylenders will offer a 'top-up' loan in this situation, but this is usually to be avoided (as we saw in Chapter 2, pp. 37–8).

Passing the debt to a solicitor

Having exhausted the computer letters or other procedure, some creditors will refer the debt to their solicitor or litigation department for legal action. Very often the solicitor is not a member of a separate independent firm instructed by the finance company but the company's own 'in-house' solicitor, who in fact often carries on using the same computer to process the debt.

Perhaps two further letters will be sent by the solicitor or litigation department. Unless there is some response from the debtor, legal proceedings will be started.

Passing the debt to a debt collection agency

There are a number of companies that specialise in debt collection. Sometimes this is the sole business of the company and there are some very large debt collection agencies. A few companies loan money themselves in addition to collecting debts for other lenders.

Many of the larger debt collection agencies use computer letters to contact defaulters. The agency is normally paid on results, i.e. it receives a proportion of the monies recovered from the debtor as payment. This can clearly tempt some agencies to use unlawful and quasi-lawful methods and can also make some debt collectors ruthless and single-minded in their approach. Debt collectors however also have to be licensed under the Consumer Credit Act 1974, so if you find one acting unscrupulously or dishonestly report them to your local Trading Standards Department or direct to the Office of Fair Trading in London.

Selling the debt to a debt collector

Some creditors actually sell the debt to a debt collection agency, by a legal device called assignment. They will pass all rights to collect the outstanding monies on to another person or company in exchange for the payment of a fee. A borrower may be in default but believes the default is with a reputable company. Suddenly the defaulter may be confronted by a less reputable debt collector pursuing the debt. Cases have arisen where defaulters have reached an agreement with the original creditor to pay off the debt at a small amount per week, and when the debt has been sold or passed to a collection agency this agreement is said to be no longer acceptable and much larger weekly sums are demanded, or even the full amount outstanding on the agreement.

Court proceedings

This is dealt with in detail in Chapter 9.

Except in the case of secured loans, most creditors regard court action as a last resort. Many do not like to go to court because of the time lost and effort involved. If a defaulter contacts the company involved, explains the problems and makes an offer (as calculated in Chapter 8), most creditors would prefer to accept that, or at least give the borrower the opportunity of honouring his agreement to repay, rather than commencing court proceedings.

Harassment

As long ago as 1970 the unlawful harassment of debtors was made a criminal offence under Section 40 of the Administration of Justice Act 1970.

A creditor commits the offence if he:

* *makes demands for payment that are so frequent or so public, or at such an inappropriate time or manner, that the demands cause the borrower or his family distress or humiliation.* This covers cases where repeated visits or telephone calls are made during the night, where visits are made to neighbours to publicise the borrower's indebtedness, where telephone calls are repeatedly made to the borrower's place of work, or calls are made to his employer or colleagues at work.

* *Untruthfully leads the borrower to believe that he can be prosecuted in the criminal courts for non-payment.*

* *Pretends to be authorised in an official capacity to claim or enforce the payment.* This covers cases where the collector wears a uniform so like that of a police officer that the borrower believes the police are involved, or where the collector pretends to be a bailiff or other officer of the court.

* *Sends a document to the debtor that pretends to be some kind of official document.* This covers cases where creditors have sent letters asking for payment which are designed to look like court documents or summonses.

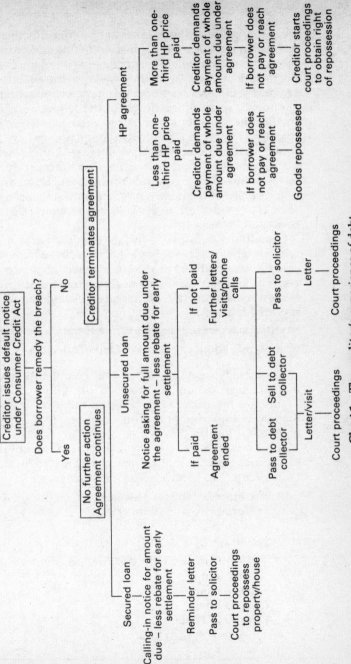

Chart 1 The creditor's experience of debt

Very few prosecutions are brought under this section because most borrowers subjected to this sort of treatment are too frightened or worried to complain. Many borrowers think that if they make a complaint the creditor will be even harder on them, or immediately commence court proceedings. In the few cases where the Birmingham Settlement Money Advice Centre has managed to persuade debtors to complain, we have not found that the creditors have increased pressure or gone straight for court proceedings; on the contrary, we have found they frequently draw back from direct enforcement of the debt. Complaint about harassment should be made both to the Trading Standards Department and to the police.

Sometimes creditors go further than the harassment set out above. There have been cases where unscrupulous creditors have threatened violence or actually used physical violence to extort money from borrowers. These are criminal offences and should be reported to the police.

Complaints about Creditors or Debt Collectors

It has already been explained that complaints about bad practice should be made to the Office of Fair Trading, either directly or through the local Trading Standards Department or Consumer Services Department of the local authority.

Some creditors belong to trade associations and it is sometimes worth complaining to such an association if your creditor is a member. The main ones are:

> The Finance Houses Association
> 18 Upper Grosvenor Street
> London W1X 9PB
> *Telephone:* 01-491 2783

> The Consumer Credit Association of the United
>   Kingdom
> Queens House
> Queens Road
> Chester CH1 3BQ
> *Telephone:* 0244 312044

The Consumer Credit Trade Association
3 Berners Street
London W1P 3AG

Telephone: 01-636 7564

The Collection Agencies Association
5 Mill Street
Bedford MK40 3EU

Some of these trade associations have codes of practice and take serious steps against members who infringe the code and/or break the law.

Conclusion

Default and debt collection are an expensive nuisance for creditors, costing time, effort and money. What most creditors want is communication from their defaulting borrowers, even if they sometimes appear to make it difficult for the borrower to get in touch. So, to get the best out of your creditor when default occurs, you need to **COMMUNICATE** with him by visit, telephone call or letter. (More detailed information on how to do so successfully is given in Chapter 8.)

Nevertheless, credit-granters really ought to look at the way they handle debtors. The fear they show of default and the often unsympathetic way they consequently treat their defaulting clients is essentially an irrational way of handling the problem. It distresses the clients, and often causes the creditor to compete with other members of his industry to collect debts. Central coordination of debt collection by creditors ought to be possible, cost effective, and, capable of treating the debtors with understanding.

4

Debt Control – What to Do to Start to Help Yourself

Being Realistic

If you are about to cross the line from being a credit user to a debtor, early action is essential. The earlier the problem is recognised and dealt with, the quicker and more effective the solutions will be.

To decide whether you need to deal with a debt problem you should first compare your household's net income with its expenditure. You then have to come to terms with the consequences of your calculation. It is surprising how many people fail to do this simple accounting exercise to work out their personal budget. To help you make your calculations, there is a Self-Help Kit at the end of the book (pp. 219–26).

During this chapter we shall use the example of John and Wendy Anderson and their family to show you how to analyse your own financial position.

The Andersons

Wendy and John are married with three children – David (19), who works as a clerk in an insurance office, and Sarah (14) and Christopher (9) who are still at school. John works as a Quality Controller for a large manufacturing company and Wendy has a small part-time job in a shop. John's mother Mary also lives with the family. She is 68 and no longer works, but is currently in good health.

They are owner-occupiers, having bought their present house six years ago. They have recently found difficulty in paying the mortgage and have mortgage arrears of £270.00 which are currently giving cause for concern.

They have also found it difficult to maintain payments on a finance company loan, and have received two arrears letters from the company concerned.

Electricity and rates bills are due soon and John and Wendy are worrying if they will be able to pay them.

Income

The first task is to calculate your *net* household income from all sources (see page 1 of Self-Help Kit). If you are paid monthly you can do your analysis on a monthly or weekly basis. If paid weekly, we suggest you work on a weekly basis. Sometimes it is advantageous to work out both weekly and monthly statements. Consider not only the income that you and your partner have coming in, but also contributions from any other member of your household towards living expenses. If you do not know how much other members of your household earn, perhaps now is the time to start having a good family talk about who earns what and how much each contributes to the household budget and why there are problems. The more you can share the problem with your family, the more it helps to solve it.

SELF-EMPLOYED
Most self-employed people have a fluctuating income and therefore the most satisfactory calculation is to look at your earnings over the last 12 months and average

them out. Remember to deduct the money you need for, or have spent on, income tax, national insurance contributions and VAT, as well as business expenses, before arriving at the net income figure.

IRREGULAR OVERTIME

If you are employed with opportunities for irregular overtime, first calculate your income on your basic pay only (i.e. the normal weekly rate). Then look at the overtime you have worked during the last six months and average it out on a weekly or monthly basis. Show this as a separate item of income, additional to your total.

If overtime is available only at certain times of the year rather than spread out over the year, do not show it in your weekly or monthly statement, but make a note at the bottom that you generally receive extra money from overtime at a particular time of the year.

The Andersons

John Anderson earns £495.00 per month net, i.e. £114.23 per week. There are occasional opportunities for overtime, which in the last 12 months amounted to £136. Wendy brings home £15 per week, and collects the Child Benefit from the Post Office. David contributes £12 per week and Mary Anderson contributes £15 weekly.

John and Wendy decide to calculate their income weekly:

Weekly income

Earnings – husband	114.23
Earnings – wife	15.00
Child Benefit	14.20
Contributions – son	12.00
– mother	15.00
	£170.43

Occasional overtime £136 per annum in March & April.

Regular Expenditure

The second task is to work out your regular household expenditure (see page 2 of the Self-Help Kit). This will include:

* housing costs

* insurance

* fuel costs

* housekeeping/milkman

* pocket money

* travel expenses

* telephone

* TV/video

* newspapers

* cigarettes

* loans and credit commitments.

These commitments arise periodically – some annually (e.g. insurance), some half-yearly (e.g. rates), some quarterly (e.g. fuel), some monthly (e.g. mortgage), some weekly (e.g. housekeeping). Ascertain how much each item costs at the time of payment, and then break it down into a monthly and/or weekly amount.

The Andersons
John and Wendy live in a four-bedroomed pre-war semi, which they are buying on mortgage, now costing £90 per month. General rates are £96.20 per half-year, water rates £49.92 per half-year. John has a life assurance policy costing £104 per annum, and house contents insurance costs £130 per year. Gas costs £49 per

summer quarter, £91.50 per winter quarter. Electricity costs £97.50 per summer quarter and £163.00 per winter quarter. John asks Wendy to work out how much she spends on a weekly basis on food, toiletries, cleaning materials, and the milkman. The Andersons own a TV and rent a video, and they have a telephone. They have newspapers delivered. John and Wendy have their own travelling expenses, plus those needed by Sarah and Christopher. Mary and David pay their own. Entertainment is difficult to assess, but John and Wendy normally go out one night a week to the local pub or the cinema. In the school holidays they might take the children on an outing, and also have the occasional meal out. They reckon £10.00 per week is about right for all these expenses. They also have four credit commitments. Their regular expenditure works out as follows:

Weekly outgoings

Mortgage	20.80	£90 per month × 12 months ÷ 52 weeks
Rates	3.70	£96.20 × 2 ÷ 52 weeks
Water rates	1.92	£49.92 × 2 ÷ 52 weeks
Life insurance	2.00	£104 ÷ 52 weeks
House contents insurance	2.50	£130 ÷ 52 weeks
Electricity	10.00	£97.50 × 2 + £163 × 2 ÷ 52 weeks
Gas	5.40	£49 × 2 + £91.50 × 2 ÷ 52 weeks
Housekeeping	67.00	
School meals	6.00	Sarah & Christopher
Pocket money	1.50	Sarah, £1; Christopher, 50p
Travelling to school	2.50	Sarah's bus pass
Travelling to work	5.60	John only
Telephone	3.00	£39 per quarter ÷ 13 weeks
TV licence	1.25	£65 ÷ 52 weeks
Video rental	3.00	£13 per month × 12 ÷ 52 weeks

Newspapers	1.40	
Entertainment	10.00	
Total	147.57	
Bank credit card	3.70	minimum payment £16 per month × 12 ÷ 52 weeks
In-store credit card	4.60	minimum payment £20 per month × 12 ÷ 52 weeks
Finance company loan	8.10	£35 per month × 12 ÷ 52 weeks
Catalogue	4.20	
TOTAL	£168.17	

So the Andersons have a weekly income of £170.43 and regular outgoings of £168.17, which looks all right. However, what they have not yet taken into account, and must, is irregular expenditure, which might throw them into deficit.

Irregular Expenditure

You cannot just consider your regular outgoings when analysing your financial position. Every household has irregular expenditure to contend with – items such as:

* clothing

* Christmas

* birthdays

* extra school expenses

* toys and books

* repairs

* decoration
* holidays
* subscriptions
* sporting activities.

These are far more difficult to work out since expenditure arises as need dictates. Try and calculate how much you spent on these and other irregular items over the last 12 months. Then divide it by 52 weeks and add it into the expenditure already calculated (see page 3 of the Self-Help Kit).

The Andersons

John and Wendy have to clothe themselves, Sarah and Christopher. Wendy buys most of the children's and her clothes through a catalogue. Shoes are bought from the High Street stores, as are the majority of John's clothes. They look back carefully over the last 12 months and calculate that they have spent:

John	100.00
Wendy	130.00
Sarah	175.00
Christopher	150.00
	£555.00

= £10.70 per week

Christmas has been a headache for Wendy this year. Trying to buy all the presents and the extra food has been very difficult. She normally spends about £10 each on presents for David and Mary, £20 each on Sarah and Christopher. She and John bought each other token presents this time, costing £10 for the two. Presents outside the immediate family for Christmas and birthdays cost £45, and she adds in an extra £15 for Christmas food and drinks.

Christmas extras	15.00
Christmas presents	
Sarah	20.00
Christopher	20.00
David	10.00
Mary	10.00
John and Wendy	10.00
Others	25.00
Birthday presents	
Sarah	20.00
Christopher	20.00
David	10.00
Mary	10.00
John and Wendy	20.00
Others	20.00
Total	£210.00

= £4.00 per week

John and Wendy are owner-occupiers who need to keep the fabric of their house in good order. They need to build into their financial analysis a savings figure for repairs and redecoration. Last year they spent £210 on redecorating the children's bedrooms. There was some routine repair work to the gutters costing £82 and some new kitchen units costing £400. Next year they will have to redecorate the living room (estimated cost £170) and do some maintenance work and retiling in the bathroom (estimate £110). In the foreseeable future the outside will need redecorating and they have been told that the drains need repairing.

Cost last year	692.00
Cost next year	280.00
	£972.00 ÷ 104 weeks

= £9.35 per week

They assess £1 per week for additional school expenses – trips, photographs, etc. – and £1 per week for health expenses, prescriptions and Wendy's spectacles.

£2.00 per week

Last year John and Wendy rented a self-catering chalet for two weeks in Devon, and took Sarah, Christopher and Mary. Mary paid her own travel costs and chipped in £50 towards the chalet rental. So the holiday cost John and Wendy:

Rental	180.00
Travel	45.00
Extras	30.00
	255.00
Less Mary's contribution	50.00
Total	£205.00

= £3.95 per week

Therefore, if John and Wendy are to retain their standard of living, they need to put by each week for irregular expenditure the following:

Clothing	10.70
Christmas/birthdays	4.00
Repairs/decoration	9.35
School expenses/ health expenses	2.00
Holidays	3.95
	£30.00

Things for the Andersons do not look too good now.

Weekly income		170.43
Regular outgoings	168.17	
Irregular outgoings	30.00	
		198.17
Deficit		£27.74 per week

The Andersons can just about manage their basic
regular expenditure, which is £2.26 less than their
income, but any irregular expenditure will push them
into debt. Some of this expenditure will be unavoid-
able so they have a problem.

You should now be able to see whether you have a debt
or potential debt problem. You may as a result be
tempted to try some of the following solutions to deal
with the problem.

Warning!
☞ Before you embark on *any* solution we suggest that you
read on and then consider the systematic approach to
debt set out in Chapters 5–8.

Solutions Debtors Often Try

Commercial borrowing

There is a great deal of advertising targeted at people with debt problems. The advertisers suggest that the way to deal with financial difficulty is to borrow more, often in the form of a 'consolidated loan plan', which gives one new loan to pay off several existing commitments. Any reborrowing or consolidated loan should be treated with great caution. Most of these loans involve swapping unsecured loans for one loan secured on an asset, normally your home.

It is very dangerous to put your house up as security. You are entering into what amounts to a second mortgage. Unless you are totally confident that you can make the repayments demanded AND that the whole of your income is completely secure, do not consider this option except as a <u>last</u> resort.

If you want to consider a consolidated loan plan, re-read Chapter 2 and ask yourself the following questions:

* will you be borrowing at a favourable rate of interest?

* is the lender a reputable credit granter?

* is there any insurance offered with the loan?

* what will the creditor do if you lose all or some of your income – will you also then lose your home?

* can you really afford the monthly repayments?

Remember!

☞ Look with especial care at any loan plan that gives you three or more months before payments commence. Interest often accrues during this period, and what seems like a breathing space is often nothing of the kind. It simply lulls you into a false belief that you have a good deal and things will be better in three months' time.

☞ Early settlement of existing loans entitles you to a rebate on the loan under the provisions of the Consumer Credit Act 1974. Make sure *you* get the benefit of the rebate and not the new credit-granter who is paying off your existing loans.

☞ Do not be tempted to borrow more than you need to repay the existing debts.

☞ Do not swap unsecured loans for secured loans except in exceptional circumstances.

☞ Never borrow money to subsidise the payment of normal outgoings. If you cannot afford your ordinary commitments, increasing them by borrowing is a very quick route to disaster.

☞ Shop around for the best deal for *your* circumstances. Speak to your building society manager before embarking on a second mortgage; he might be able to offer you more favourable terms. Take independent advice if it is available, from a money advice centre, law centre, Citizens' or Consumer Advice Bureau.

Borrowing from family and friends
In an emergency this is a solution that many debtors consider. However it is worth remembering that borrowing from relatives or friends can create tensions, jealousy and disagreement, and ultimately destroy relationships.

Remember!
☞ Tell the truth from the outset. Inform your friend or relative of the true level of your indebtedness, your income and expenditure position and the reason why you want the loan. This will enable your lender to make an informed decision whether or not to lend you the money in the first place.

☞ Be prepared for them to say 'no' or to hesitate. You may not know the full details of their financial position.

☞ Do not ask them to borrow money on your behalf.

☞ To avoid misunderstandings and arguments later, put the details of the loan agreement in writing, setting out the amount borrowed and the repayment terms.

☞ Do not be tempted to make unrealistic promises of repayment; it will only cause problems later.

☞ Keep the relative or friend in the picture with up-to-date information. Do not make them ask.

Even if you do not want to borrow from close friends and family, it is a good idea to tell them about your temporary difficulties, so that they understand that you are not being mean, ungenerous or anti-social, but that you are trying to take care with income and expenditure in a period of difficulty.

Selling an asset
The most valuable realisable assets are likely to be your home and/or your car. Selling either to pay debts can cause further problems of homelessness or transport difficulties. So carefully consider the consequences before embarking on such a course.

Trading down (i.e. buying something cheaper) can be a solution, but you need to satisfy yourself that after paying all the costs of sale and removal expenses you are gaining sufficient capital to make the upheaval and inconvenience worthwhile. You also need to be sure that this will solve the problem. Trading down with a house or car may involve purchasing an older property or vehicle that will need more maintenance than the one you already have, thus increasing your expenditure. Carefully consider what your future income and outgoings will be when living in a new property or using an alternative means of transport.

You may have other assets which you are thinking of selling – pictures, silver, antique furniture, china, porcelain, jewellery, and so on.

Remember!

☞ Get several quotations from different dealers before actually parting with your goods.

☞ Get paid in cash.

☞ Never sell to people who come knocking at the door asking for items.

☞ If you have no idea of the value of a particular piece, contact a local auction house or the local branch of one of the national auction houses for a free valuation.

Cashing insurance policies

If you have one or several insurance policies you may have thought of cashing in the policies early to raise capital. Before doing so consult a reputable insurance broker or your bank manager. Sometimes it is not a cost-effective option since the capital sum raised could be less than the instalments paid to date.

Robbing Peter to pay Paul

This is a course that many debtors use in the early days of their financial difficulties. Missing a payment here or there can appear to be a satisfactory way of juggling competing commitments. **Do not do this.** It is never a solution and usually produces multiple debts instead of a single debt problem.

If you find you are missing the mortgage or rent so that you can pay for your fuel, or that you are missing your general rate payment so that you can pay your finance company, you have a debt problem that needs controlling.

Disappearing

If financial problems become really desperate, debtors may be tempted to walk away from their problems, persuading themselves that a fresh start in a new environment is the answer. This is not a satisfactory solution since it cheats the creditor who has lent money in good faith. In addition, the debtor will always be looking over his shoulder wondering when the debts and the creditor will catch up with him. If the creditor does trace the debtor, he will never trust him again and the debtor will have lost all credibility.

This is not a realistic solution.

Buying time with creditors
This is a course that many debtors use in dealings with their creditors. They make promises of payment that realistically cannot be fulfilled in an effort to 'buy time'. This is a destructive tactic because creditors find broken promises extremely annoying. The creditor who has expended time, effort and resources contacting the debtor, and who then finds he has to repeat the exercise when the promised money is not forthcoming, is going to be a difficult creditor in any future negotiations.

It is always better to be frank with creditors from the start and not to make unrealistic offers. Offers to creditors need to be calculated in the systematic way set out in the next few chapters.

The Systematic Approach

We believe the systematic approach is more likely to provide you with a satisfactory solution. In essence this approach looks first at your ordinary income and outgoings and how they can be changed for the better (Chapter 5 and 6). The aim is to see how much you need to live on without your debts. At the end of this exercise you will have a budget for the future that will relate expenditure to income. You will be at least in a break-even position on your budget so that you cannot drift into further debts. We call this future budget your **Financial Statement** (see pages 4–8 of the Self-Help Kit).

We then see how to deal with the debts you have

from the past with the money you have available for the future (Chapters 7 and 8).

The importance of the Financial Statement
The Financial Statement you will be preparing should become the most important tool in rebuilding your finances.

* It is your guide in your attempts to control future spending.

* It is the document that you can send to creditors giving a concise picture of your financial position.

* It is the document that will justify offers of repayment that you make to creditors.

* If you find yourself involved in court proceedings as a result of debt, it is the document that you can send to the court, or present at the hearing to show income and expenditure at a glance.

The Financial Statement may need to be readjusted if income or expenditure changes, so it is important to review your financial performance from time to time and make corrections accordingly. As you start to negotiate agreements with creditors, these payments can be added into your Financial Statement so that debts from the past get paid alongside day-to-day commitments.

5

Maximising Your Income

When you have financial problems, one of the most important things to do is look at your income. You must be sure you are acquiring all the money you can for your household, and you have to be systematic about it. The job is called *income maximisation*.

There are three reasons for undertaking this exercise:

* In any negotiations with your creditors you will need a *Financial Statement* showing your income and outgoings. You will have to list all the sources of your income and how much you receive from each source. Since you have to do this, it makes sense to check that you are getting as much as you may be entitled to.

* Many people have a vague feeling that they are short somewhere or could be receiving more, but since they do not keep a list of all sources of income it is not easy to check. This is an opportunity to satisfy yourself that you are, in fact, getting in all you can.

* You just might find you are entitled to, or can earn, some extra money and this would certainly help with any financial problems.

Increasing Your Household's Earnings

There are four main ways of increasing the earned income of your household:

● checking your income tax

● improving a low wage

● taking additional part-time work yourself

● your partner working or recommencing work.

Income tax – are you paying too much?
The UK income tax system is fairly simple. **Employed people** pay tax on their earnings under Pay As You Earn (PAYE), whereby tax is deducted by your employer before you get your pay packet and paid to the Inland Revenue (tax office) for you (superannuation and pension payments are not taxed). Your employer deducts your tax according to a code number given by your tax office. Your code number is calculated from the information you give when you fill in a Tax Return. From that information the Inland Revenue decide what allowances and tax relief you are entitled to and what rate of tax you must pay. The code is simply the first three numbers of your total allowances.

ALLOWANCES
There are three basic personal allowances:

* single person's allowance

* married man's allowance

* married woman's earned income allowance.

There are no tax allowances for children – you receive Child Benefit instead.

Additional allowances, which are still part of the tax code, are available if you have a dependent relative, if you have special expenses as a result of your job, or if you or your partner has to care for a handicapped person.

TAX RELIEF

If you have a mortgage you can claim tax relief on your interest payments on up to £30,000 of mortgage through a scheme called MIRAS (Mortgage Interest Relief at Source). Home-owners with second mortgages or home improvement loans are often entitled to tax relief on these monthly payments. If you have taken out a loan to extend or improve your home, it is well worth checking with your local tax office whether you are entitled to income tax relief on these repayments. You will find the address and telephone number in the telephone directory under 'Inland Revenue'.

☞ The first thing to do therefore is to check your tax code. Each year you should receive a Notice of Coding and the code should also be on your pay slip.

If you think your tax code is incorrect you need to write to, visit or phone the tax office that deals with

> Examples of a tax code
>
> John Anderson is a married man with no extra allowances. The married man's tax allowance is £3,655 in 1986/87, and so his code is 365.
>
> Wendy Anderson, his wife, gets the married woman's earned income allowance, which is £2,335 in 1986/87. Her tax code is thus 233.
>
> Wendy's brother is a single man but gives his mother £3 a week, which she needs as she is very old. He gets the single man's tax allowance of £2,335 plus the dependent relative allowance of £100 (the maximum), so his code is 243.

your employer (and therefore also you), asking whether you are entitled to an allowance for something not included. If it is agreed that there has been a mistake, you should ask for your tax code to be changed and for the change to be backdated to recover the tax that you have overpaid. Payment can be backdated for up to seven years.

Self-employed people are directly responsible for payment of their own tax to the Inland Revenue. They are entitled to the same allowances as employed people, but the situation is more complicated because of the need to calculate allowable business expenses. The most important task, if you are self-employed, is to keep very careful records of all your earnings and all the costs incurred whilst running your business. These records are the basis of a claim for allowances from the tax office and if they are not kept can lead to lengthy disputes and loss of income to the tax authorities.

Self-employed people are also well advised to set aside some money each month out of their gross receipts for their income tax and national insurance contributions. If registered for VAT it is also wise to provide for that. Failure to do so has led many self-employed people into trouble. If you are already facing these difficulties, start remedying your position now. A good rule of thumb is to put 30 per cent of gross receipts in a separate account in the bank or building society where it can earn interest until the time comes to pay.

If you are self-employed or contemplating self-employment, it is worth obtaining the services of a reputable chartered accountant as soon as possible. For a fairly modest fee, deductable against tax, he will:

* prepare your business accounts,

* negotiate with the tax authorities on your behalf,

* advise you on what tax allowances and expenses you can claim or are deductable,

* advise you on the most efficient way of running your business.

If you are **unmarried and cohabiting** with a partner, your tax position needs looking at very carefully. A man is not normally entitled to the higher married man's tax allowance even if his partner is dependent upon him. If, however, there are dependent children within the household, there is an additional personal allowance that can be claimed while caring for them. You should seek the advice of your tax office in claiming this allowance.

Single parents are also entitled to an additional tax allowance while they are caring for their children.

If in a marriage **the wife is working** and the man is unemployed, it is usually possible to transfer the un-used part of the higher married man's allowance to the wife.

If you and your husband or wife jointly earn over a certain amount (£16,200 in 1985/86) so that you are liable to pay tax at more than the standard rate, it may be worthwhile applying for separate assessment. This reduces the total amount of income that is taxable by treating both of you as single people.

The Inland Revenue publish a number of information leaflets describing the different tax positions of various types of taxpayer. It is worth visiting your local tax office to see if they have one to fit your circumstances. Recently unemployed people anticipating a tax refund would be particularly well advised to do so.

The Inland Revenue also offer a phone-in service, whereby you can put your position to the tax officer, without letting him know who you are if you wish, and get first-hand advice. This is usually a fast and accurate service. You can find the number to call in the telephone directory under 'Inland Revenue'.

Low wages
How do you decide whether your job is 'low-waged'? Various definitions have been given and if you find

yourself in one of the following situations you can consider yourself in receipt of a low wage:

* taking home less than £115 per week

* earning less than you would be entitled to on social security

* receiving only £10–15 per week more from your job than you would be entitled to on social security

* working in poor conditions, which are not recognised in extra pay

* working unsocial hours, which are not reflected in higher wage rates.

If you fall into one or more of these categories, you should read this section, and also pp. 85–90 of this chapter on state benefits, since you may also be entitled to financial assistance through Housing Benefit, Supplementary Benefit or Family Income Supplement.

Some trades that have traditionally been associated with low pay (e.g. hairdressing, catering) are now covered by 'Wages Council Orders' which set a minimum wage for the job. For those trades covered by such agreements, and the minimum wages involved, check with the Wages Inspectorate or ACAS (Advisory Conciliation and Arbitration Service), the telephone number and address of which will be in the telephone directory.

If you work in very poor conditions, and feel the pay does not reflect this and/or the conditions need to be improved, you should consider joining an appropriate trades union which can sometimes negotiate for you. There will be real problems with this approach, however, if most of your fellow employees are unwilling to act with you and your employer is hostile. It may be best to consult a trades union official confidentially at first for advice.

One final solution might be to seek better-paid work if you can. It may take a long time to find another job and it is important not to give up your present one, but sometimes it is the only way in the long run to improve your income.

Part-time work
Although we live in a society where unemployment is a major problem, many people do find small part-time jobs in addition to their main job, which add much-needed income to their weekly or monthly budgets. Many of these jobs are in restaurants, public houses, garages, shops and at weekends in leisure centres. Cleaners are usually part-time, as are many gardeners and baby-sitters. You should consider whether you can take up a part-time job to help out while you have financial problems, particularly if you are in low-paid work.

If you are unemployed and unable to find full-time work, you might consider getting a part-time job. A part-time job can be an important morale booster, can provide vital extra income, and can often be the route back into full-time work. You may be limited in how much work you can accept, since extra earnings can affect entitlement to state benefits, particularly Supplementary Benefit. Before accepting part-time employment, check with the DHSS or an advice agency such as the Citizens' Advice Bureau how it will affect your benefit position.

Remember!
If you earn money and fail to tell the authorities whilst claiming, you may be committing a criminal offence, and run the risk of being prosecuted.

Partner's earnings
Debt problems very often arise or worsen when one partner in a household leaves work. If the reason is to start a family, it means that, instead of having two incomes to keep two people, one income must now keep three. It is advisable to consider very carefully in advance whether or not a partner should give up work.

It can be difficult for both partners to work full-time or part-time when there are children, especially young children, in the family, but it needs to be considered as an option when you have financial problems.

The first task is to work out the logistics. The hours a non-working partner could work will depend upon whether the children are at school or not, the availability of childcare or nurseries, the hours of work of the working partner and the cost of arranging childcare. Many of the jobs mentioned as frequently available for part-time work could be considered in these circumstances. It may be possible to work at home, as skilled typists sometimes do. However, some 'home work' is very badly paid, and should not be undertaken without careful thought. This is particularly true if you are thinking of responding to an advertisement that promises great earnings but requires a capital outlay first to buy stock or expertise.

Equally vital is to work out the net financial gain. Any anticipated income must be balanced against necessary costs such as childminding, travelling and possible outlay for clothing or equipment. If the gain is fairly small, you also need to be sure the cost in energy and personal effort is worth it.

State Benefits

Many people live on state benefits or rely upon them for part of their income. This section is not a comprehensive guide, but indicates which areas should be checked. The Department of Health and Social Security publish a whole range of leaflets explaining benefits in detail and these should be available in your local DHSS office, Citizens' Advice Bureau or community centre.

Note
The state benefits system is presently being changed by the government, and these changes will be implemented in 1987/8. We have tried to indicate how individual benefits mentioned here may be altered.

Family Income Supplement (FIS)
This is a benefit paid by central government through the Department of Health and Social Security to low-income earners who have one or more children living in their household. Married couples, co-habitees and single parents qualify, provided that they are working a minimum number of hours per week.

The benefit is calculated on the gross income of the family and on the number of children living within the family. The assessment levels are increased annually. If your gross income (including maintenance) is in the region of £5,000 per annum, or more if you have more than one child, you should consider claiming.

☞ To claim FIS, obtain Form FIS.1 from your local Post Office or DHSS office.

Once you have successfully claimed FIS, you receive it for 12 months even if your circumstances change. Receipt of FIS entitles you to other benefits such as free school meals and free prescriptions, although these additional entitlements are presently under review by the government.

At the time of going to press, it is proposed to replace FIS with Family Credits, which will be paid to the wage earner through the wage packet.

Housing Benefit
The Housing Benefit scheme was introduced between November 1982 and April 1983 to replace the old system of rent and rate rebates. It has proved complicated and unwieldy to administer and has resulted in huge delays in the processing of applications and in large amounts of benefit going unclaimed. The delays themselves often get people into debt and rent arrears.

The essence of Housing Benefit is to provide assistance with rent and rates for tenants with low incomes, or assistance with rates for owner-occupiers with low incomes. Retirement pensioners, employed, unemployed and self-employed people can claim.

☞ Claim forms are available from your local authority Housing Department.

Supplementary Benefit
The legislation controlling entitlement to Supplementary Benefit is lengthy and complex. Many people who are entitled to it fail to claim.

Both employed and unemployed people can qualify for Supplementary Benefit. It is a means-tested benefit and entitlement depends on both income and capital resources.

Benefit is divided into three categories:

● basic requirements

● housing requirements

● additional requirements.

Basic requirements provide rates of weekly benefit to cover food, fuel, clothing, travelling and general living expenses. These are fixed rates reviewed annually by Parliament and do not reflect your actual expenditure on these items.

Housing requirements cover:

* *For tenants* – rent and rates (where not covered by Housing Benefit) and water rates.

* For owner-occupiers – the *interest* portion of the mortgage repayment, rates (where not covered by Housing Benefit), and water rates. *Also* an allowance for insurance and maintenance. *Also*, in certain circumstances, the interest portion of repayments on a second mortgage, or a loan for repairs and house improvements.

Additional requirements cover any special needs you may have in areas such as:

* special diet

* extra baths

* extra heating

* laundry

* hire purchase (in certain circumstances)

* hospital fares.

☞ To claim Supplementary Benefit, obtain Form S.B.1 from your local DHSS office or Post Office.

When you are in receipt of Supplementary Benefit you may also be able to apply for one-off grants called **'single payments'** if you need an item that the regulations cover, e.g.

* baby things

* bedding

* furniture and household equipment

* removal expenses

* goods on hire purchase

* repairs and redecoration

* fuel bills (in special circumstances)

* funeral expenses.

Receipt of Supplementary Benefit also entitles you to other benefits, e.g.

* free school meals

* free prescriptions

* free dental treatment

* milk tokens

The government intend to introduce new legislation to abolish Supplementary Benefit and replace it by an entirely new benefit called Income Support. This will provide a set rate to cover all outgoings, with some extra help to cover housing costs, although exactly what has not yet been finalised. Additional requirements and single payments will no longer be available. They will be replaced by a discretionary grant and loan system called the Social Fund. It will be cash limited each year, so the money may run out towards the end of the year. Many believe that under the new Income Support system present Supplementary Benefit claimants will have less money.

Other social security benefits
In addition to the three benefits listed above, there are other social security benefits to which you become entitled as of right, irrespective of your means, when certain circumstances occur. Examples of 'circumstance' non-means tested benefits are:

- Unemployment Benefit

- Sickness Benefit

- Invalidity Benefit

- Severe Disablement Allowance

- Maternity Allowance

- Maternity Grant

- Invalidity Allowance

- Widow's Benefits

- Retirement Pension

- Mobility Allowance

● Attendance Allowance

● Invalid Care Allowance

● Child Benefit

☞ If you think you may be entitled to one or more of these benefits, check with your local DHSS office or Citizens' Advice Bureau.

Further information on all state benefits can be obtained by reading the excellent Child Poverty Action Group publications:

* *National Welfare Benefits Handbook*
* *Rights Guide to Non-Means Tested Social Security Benefits*

These books are published annually and will deal with new legislation as it occurs. They are obtainable from CPAG, 1 Macklin Street, London WC2B 5NH.

Income from Other Members of Your Household

Lodgers
Taking a lodger can be a useful way of spreading the costs of running a house that has become too big for you. It can also provide welcome company for those living alone.

University and college students sometimes prefer to lodge rather than rent their own property. Contact the Student Accommodation Office of your local university or college for further information. More mature lodgers can be found amongst people working away from home, who frequently require lodgings during the week only.

Before taking a lodger you should check with your mortgage-granter or landlord that you are not infringing any agreement you have.

Always fix a realistic contribution for the lodger to pay, otherwise taking a lodger will not provide the extra income which you need.

Remember!
Income from a lodger is taxable, but only after allowance has been made for:

* a proportion of the housing costs,

* a proportion of the fuel costs,

* the cost of feeding the lodger,

* wear and tear on furniture.

> Further information about the tax position can be obtained from your local Inland Revenue office.
>
> Further information about the legal aspects can be obtained from a law centre or solicitor. Always use a solicitor who offers help under the legal aid scheme.

Non-dependants
If you take a lodger into your house, you expect him to pay his way. The same should apply to any grown-up children or elderly relatives living with you. Financial difficulties can arise where a non-dependant fails to contribute a realistic amount to household expenses, so that the householder is in effect subsidising the non-dependant's living expenses.

This is a very sensitive area which is sometimes not discussed in families, leaving the non-dependant to pay into the household budget what he feels is appropriate and not a sum that has been carefully calculated to reflect actual costs.

If you have a non-dependant living in your household, work out what the contribution should be, as set out in the following example:

Tom and Brenda Griffiths have two children, Robert (22) and Nicola (18), both still living at home. Robert is working; Nicola has just lost her job and is living on social security benefits.

The basic weekly household budget is as follows:

Housing costs (mortgage, rates, water rates)	51.00
Fuel (gas and electricity)	15.00
Food	45.00
TV licence/telephone	3.00
	£114.00
=	£28.50 per person

Tom and Brenda know that if Nicola and Robert were not living at home they would still have the same housing costs; however, they cannot move to a smaller property until Robert and Nicola leave home, and so would like to ask for a small contribution towards housing costs.

Fuel	15.00
Food	45.00
Other	3.00
	£63.00 ÷ 4
=	£15.75
Plus housing costs	5.00
Non-dependant contribution =	**£20.75**

Robert can easily afford this amount because he is earning £65.00 per week net. Nicola is in receipt of supplementary benefit of £23.85 and cannot. Tom and Brenda cannot afford to subsidise Nicola, but realise that she needs around £12 per week for her personal expenditure, i.e.

Clothing	4.00
Travelling	3.00
Entertainment	4.00
Toiletries, make-up, etc.	1.00
	£12.00

The family decide that it would be fair to discount Nicola's contribution to £11.50 per week until she finds another job.

If your non-dependant is an elderly relative in receipt of a retirement pension, similar considerations apply.

If your non-dependant refuses to make a realistic contribution, even when you have explained the basis upon which you have calculated your request, the intervention of a third party whom your non-dependant respects may be helpful.

There are rare cases where non-dependants refuse to pay anything. In these circumstances you can ask them to leave or cease providing them with food, laundry and other services. We hope that this drastic action will not be necessary, but remember you do have considerable rights in this situation. What is also on your side is that it will certainly cost them more if they leave to set up their own home.

Separation and Divorce

Income tax
Separation and divorce can affect the tax position of

both partners, particularly where they have been
married:

* A husband will lose his married man's personal allowance at the end of the financial year in which he leaves
his wife.

* A separated or divorced single parent is entitled to an
additional personal allowance when caring for dependent children.

* A partner paying maintenance payments can claim
extra tax relief in certain circumstances. Maintenance
payments are taxable in the hands of the recipient, so
any payments made for the maintenance of children
should be made payable *not* to the caring adult but to
the child.

**Further information can be gained from your local
income tax office, by consulting your matrimonial
lawyer, if you have one, or by paying to see a chartered
accountant.**

You could also usefully read Anthony Hetherington's
book *How to Split up – and survive financially* (published by Allen & Unwin).

Irregular maintenance

THE RECIPIENT
Irregular maintenance payments cause the recipient
great problems. It is impossible to budget accurately
when you do not know whether a substantial part of
your income will actually be paid. Consider these
options:

* If the person who pays you maintenance is working,
you can apply to the court for an attachment of earnings
order whereby your payments are deducted by the
payer's employers from his earnings and paid direct
into court.

* If you are in receipt of Supplementary Benefit and irregular maintenance is affecting your entitlement, you can ask the DHSS to collect the maintenance on your behalf and they will then pay you your full entitlement.

* If you are working and earning enough to pay income tax, make sure you are not being charged tax on maintenance payments that you have not received.

* Discuss the matter with a lawyer specialising in matrimonial law.

THE PAYER
If you have been ordered to pay maintenance and find that you cannot afford to make the payments regularly, you should consider these options:

* Make an application to the court for the maintenance payments to be reduced. There are two grounds for making such an application:

    ● your income has reduced
    ● your outgoings have increased.

The court will fix a hearing. Be prepared to argue your case by providing the court with full information on your income and outgoings.

* Make an application to the court for an attachment of earnings order so that your earnings are paid to you net of maintenance and your employer makes a direct payment into court.

* Check that you are making the maintenance payments in the most tax-efficient way.

* If you are unemployed, apply to the court for the payments to be reduced to a nominal amount because you will only be able to claim state benefits as a single person.

Child Benefit

Most single, separated or divorced people who are caring for a child or children are entitled to an additional One-Parent Child Benefit. This cannot be claimed if you are residing with someone as if you were husband and wife.

Miscellaneous Points

Staff welfare funds

Some large employers have set up staff welfare funds to provide financial help to employees with difficulties. These have proved very valuable in cases of severe hardship, where for example eviction or disconnection was threatened. In an appropriate case they will make either a one-off grant or an interest-free loan to pay debts.

If you are in severe financial difficulty you can find out whether such a fund exists from your Staff Welfare Officer or Personnel Manager, who should also be able to tell you of the criteria for payment. Occasionally a small employer will help out even though no staff welfare fund exists. If you have a problem an employer might help you with and are in good standing as an employee, it might be worth asking for help.

Charities

There are a number of charities that have funds available for the relief of hardship and poverty. They will be pleased to hear from you since large sums of money often go unclaimed. Your enquiry will be treated in confidence and with care and sympathy. Don't be ashamed to ask.

If you wish to investigate this possibility look in your local library at the Register of Charities or enquire at your local Citizens' Advice Bureau for further information.

If you have served in the armed forces, the Soldiers, Sailors and Airforce Association can sometimes help.

Selling an asset
See Chapter 4 (p. 74).

Cashing insurance policies
See Chapter 4 (p. 75).

Contributions from friends or relatives
When financial difficulties occur, a common reaction is to hide the fact from relatives and friends, so that you can 'keep your heads up' in society. However, relatives and friends may be anxious to help out, not perhaps by lending a lump sum but by paying a specific outgoing for you, as in the following example.

> Robert White lost his job and realised that he could not afford to keep the telephone. His wife, Janet, was really concerned because, although part of a large family, she was the only child living in the same area as her elderly, now disabled, father. He lived alone and relied on the telephone to contact Janet in the event of an emergency. She wanted to keep the security of the phone so she could telephone him periodically to make sure everything was all right. Janet's brother lived 200 miles away and could not care for his father. When he heard about Robert's job loss he offered to pay for the telephone.

Education grants
In some parts of the country the local authority education department offers education grants for low-income families with school-aged children. The grant may assist

with travelling to school, school dinners, school uniform and additional school activities such as music lessons.

Further information can be obtained from your local authority Education Department.

Special Cases

Students
If any of your children are in full-time further education at college or university, and you are continuing to support them to some extent, and if you are a tax payer, you should investigate the possibility of arranging a covenant. This means that you sign an agreement undertaking to pay your child a fixed sum each year for several years. The sums paid must be less than your child's personal allowance for tax purposes. Your child can then recover from the Inland Revenue the tax that you have already paid on the amount covenanted. For example:

> Brian and Valerie Green have two children at university. Brian is working and pays tax at the standard rate. He covenants to pay each child £600 per annum. He pays £426 to each child. Each child can then recover £174 from the Inland Revenue. The income is not taxable in their hands because it is less than their single person's allowance.

 If you have any child involved in further education, you should enquire from your local authority Education Department what grants are available.

The disabled and elderly
There are benefits and services available to disabled

and elderly people that can increase income or reduce
expenditure. The main examples are:

* Mobility Allowance

* Attendance Allowance

* home-help schemes

* meals on wheels

* day-care centres.

**Further information can be obtained from your DHSS
office, local authority, or Citizens' Advice Bureau.**

Casual earnings – the black economy
It would be naive to ignore the effect of the black
economy on people's income. Casual earnings, un-
declared to the Inland Revenue and DHSS, are a
method that some debtors, not to mention others, use
as a means of maximising income. The practice has
various names in different parts of the country to
describe different circumstances – 'moonlighting',
'doing a foreigner', for example. Some part-time work
is undertaken in this way.
 It is perfectly lawful to earn money through working
casually, provided that:

* national insurance contributions are paid;

* a declaration of earnings is made to the Inland Revenue;

* a declaration is made to the DHSS when claiming social
security benefits;

* a declaration is made to the local authority Housing
Department when claiming Housing Benefit.

If you hide casual earnings from these authorities you
may be committing a criminal offence, which could

involve you in a prosecution and appearance before the criminal courts.

Further difficulties can arise when negotiating with creditors. Regular casual earnings would have to be shown in the income section of your Financial Statement since it is essential to present a true picture of your total income from all sources to your creditors. This could prove awkward if you are attempting to conceal such earnings from the DHSS or Inland Revenue.

Remember!
Involvement in the black economy may be widespread, but is a risky business. Think very carefully about the disadvantages and the consequences of unlawful action if you are tempted to pursue such a course.

Checklist
☞ income tax personal allowances, mortgage interest relief at source (MIRAS)

☞ self-employed tax position

☞ separated, divorced and cohabiting tax position

☞ irregular maintenance

☞ transfer of married man's allowance to working wife

☞ separate taxation of wife's earnings

☞ welfare benefit entitlement

☞ FIS (Family Income Supplement)

☞ Housing Benefit

☞ Supplementary Benefit

☞ Wages Council Agreement

☞ trades union involvement

☞ part-time work

☞ partner's earnings

☞ lodgers

☞ non-dependant contribution

☞ staff welfare funds

☞ charities

☞ contributions from friends and relatives

☞ covenants for students

☞ education grants

☞ special provision for the elderly and disabled.

You should now be in a position to fill in Part I of your Financial Statement (Self-Help Kit, p. 4).

The Andersons

John and Wendy look at ways of maximising their income. John checks his tax code and finds that it is correct. Wendy asks her employer whether she can work any more hours. Unfortunately he says 'no'. They are earning too much between them to be entitled to any state benefits.

The area where they find they can improve their income is the sensitive one of David's and Mary's contributions. They work out that the actual cost to the household of David is £20.00 per week and of Mary is £17.50 per week. They have a family discussion and David and Mary both agree to increase their contributions. They are both quite shocked to hear that the family is in financial difficulty and particularly that the mortgage is in arrears. Neither David nor Mary had really thought about how much they were contributing, and are both anxious to do what they can to help. This increases the Andersons' weekly income to £180.93.

6

Essential Outgoings

If your outgoings exceed your income, then you have a debt problem. In this chapter we take a more detailed look at expenditure as part of the task of trying to find a solution. We try to point out the kind of hard decisions that have to be taken to decide which outgoings are essential, and therefore cannot be reduced, and which outgoings can be looked at again, and either reduced or eliminated.

As part of this task we shall need to examine how you pay for essentials as well as how much they cost. Irregular payments of large sums each quarter can be difficult if you are on a tight budget, whereas small amounts paid regularly are easier to cope with.

By the end of this chapter we should be able to complete your Financial Statement (see pages 4–8 of the Self-Help Kit), which will be your financial blueprint for the future. Our task is to find a way to bring your income and expenditure into balance, with, we hope, some surplus income that can then be used to start paying your debts. This surplus we shall call your 'disposable income'.

We shall be following the fortunes of the Anderson family again as an example.

Dividing Your Expenditure into Four Categories

To enable you to decide what your spending priorities are, we recommend you divide expenditure into four categories:

● *Category 1*   Your basic essential outgoings that are easy to quantify, such as housing, fuel, food and travel to work.

● *Category 2*   Other essentials that are difficult to quantify because they arise irregularly, such as clothing, repairs and health expenses.

● *Category 3*   Items of expenditure that may be considered as the extras of life or luxuries, such as meals out, alcohol, cigarettes, gambling and video rental.

● *Category 4*   Your consumer credit commitments and money that you owe on items or services already purchased or consumed.

These categories have been developed by the Birmingham Settlement Money Advice Centre after 15 years of experience in giving practical advice to debtors. They are designed as a guide rather than as set categories into which a named item of expenditure has to fit. They can overlap, since it is sometimes hard to decide which category some expenditure should be in, as we shall see. The idea is to make sure you distinguish what has to be paid each week or month to ensure your future financial security, and what you can do without.

We shall now examine the specific items you will have to include in each of your first three categories of expenditure. Again these will not be comprehensive lists, but guidelines. With the possible exception of hire purchase payments on essential items (see Chapter 7, p. 146), category 4 items are debts rather than outgoings, so we shall deal with them when we try to come to terms with your creditors (Chapters 7 and 8). We shall build them in to the Financial Statement when we see how much disposable income is available for payment of debts and when debts have been prioritised.

Category 1 – Basic Essentials Easy to Quantify

Your main essentials are likely to be:

* *Housing*
  * mortgage
  * second mortgage
  * rent
  * rates
  * water rates
  * ground rent (if any)

* *Fuel*
  * gas
  * electricity
  * calor gas
  * coal
  * paraffin
  * oil

* *Housekeeping*
  * food
  * toiletries
  * cleaning materials
  * milkman

* *Insurance*
  * life insurance
  * house insurance
  * house contents insurance

* *Children*
  * childminding
  * school meals
  * pocket money

* *Miscellaneous*
  * travelling expenses
  * fines

- maintenance payments
- TV rental
- TV licence
- laundry/launderette

☞ Work out how much these items are costing you on a weekly basis (see Chapter 4, pp. 65–7). If you wish, you can then go on to consider them on a monthly basis.

When these items are included in your Financial Statement you must be prepared to justify your expenditure should any query arise. Most of this expenditure is fixed and therefore cannot be challenged by creditors, but problems can occur with some items.

Housekeeping
It is very difficult to set down hard and fast rules suggesting how much a particular household should spend on housekeeping. Expenditure will depend on the ages of the members of the household, whether there are any special diet requirements, whether there is access to cheaper shops, and other imponderables. The most important factor when considering housekeeping is to arrive at a figure that is reasonable for your family and then keep expenditure within that figure. When quantifying your expenditure on housekeeping, it is important to include not only the cost of food, but also such items as cleaning materials, toiletries, toothpaste, sweets and pet food.

It is our experience that people who are living through financial difficulties often reduce expenditure on food too much. With some hesitation we suggest the following rough guidelines as minimum figures:

Single person	£15 per week
2 person household	£25 per week
3 person household	£35 per week
4 person household	£45 per week
5 person household	£55 per week

If you are spending less than this and feeding your household adequately – congratulations. Some vegetarians, for example, do manage on considerably less. If you are spending a lot more than these figures and there are no special requirements in your household, perhaps a further examination of your spending is advisable.

Insurance

Everyone acknowledges that insuring the fabric of your house and the contents is important. Failure to do so can lead to very serious consequences in the event of fire or burglary. If possible arrange to pay the premiums weekly or monthly rather than annually.

Life insurance is a more difficult area. Whilst it is important to protect your spouse and children in the event of your death, it may be difficult to justify large premiums to your unpaid creditors. If you are spending more than one-thirtieth of your total net income on life insurance, you should contact your insurance company or broker and discuss ways of reducing this commitment, at least in the short term.

Travelling expenses

Travelling expenses to work, school and the shops should be included. If you are using public transport, there can be no query on your expenses, but problems can arise if you live in an area with good public transport and you are running a vehicle.

When quantifying expenditure you must include not only petrol and oil, but also:

* the road fund licence (car tax)

* car insurance (it is an offence to drive without insurance)

* the cost of servicing

* repairs and maintenance

* MOT expenses

*   hire purchase instalments if your vehicle is on HP.

All these expenses added together are likely to produce a very large figure. Therefore, unless you can establish that:

● you need the vehicle to get to work or in the course of your work

AND

● public transport is inappropriate because of the amount of travel you undertake, or unsocial hours, or the lack of public transport,

you may have a great deal of difficulty justifying the expense of running a vehicle to your creditors. If the weekly costs of running a vehicle amount to more than one-tenth of your weekly net income, you need to think seriously about keeping your car.

Television

It is commonly accepted that a television is an essential feature of most households – 97 per cent of households in the United Kingdom possess a television. It is a very cheap form of entertainment for adults and children, and viewing together is a modern social family occupation. Justifying the expense of a television rental, plus licence, to a creditor should not be a major problem. Paying for the licence may pose problems, however. TV licence stamps can be purchased from the Post Office.

Remember!

A licence is essential, otherwise prosecution and a fine may follow.

How to pay

MORTGAGES

Monthly payment is the norm, preferably by monthly standing order from your bank account. However, if you are paid weekly, or have no bank account, managing payment is likely to be more difficult. In these circumstances you should discuss the question with your mortgage-granter. If the company has a branch close to where you live, it may be possible for you to pay weekly by cash.

RENT

Contractual payment for rent may be weekly, fortnightly, monthly, quarterly, or annually. For our purposes weekly or monthly payments are most advantageous, because most people are paid weekly or monthly, and most public sector landlords such as local authorities and housing associations are prepared to accept weekly payments.

GENERAL AND WATER RATES

These fall due in April and October. Most local authorities and water boards will now take monthly instalments to spread the load. You should ask whether payments are calculated over 10 or 12 months, how much the payments will be, and for a payment book if appropriate.

GAS AND ELECTRICITY

These are normally provided on a quarterly account basis, which means that a bill is issued at three-monthly intervals for fuel consumed in the previous 13 weeks. If a meter reading cannot be taken an estimated bill is sent. Alternative methods of payment are:

* slot meter,

* pay-as-you-go-schemes, weekly or monthly,

* savings stamps for fuel,

* direct payment by DHSS for those in receipt of Supplementary Benefit.

If you are up to date with your fuel payments, the best option to consider is the 'pay-as-you-go' scheme. If you have a fuel bill, or are expecting one in the near future, that you cannot pay, insert a figure in your Financial Statement for on-going consumption as described on page 66 and turn to Chapter 7, pp. 136–42, for more detailed consideration of fuel debts.

TV LICENCE
The demand for payment of the TV licence arrives annually, but it is possible to purchase TV licence stamps weekly from the Post Office to spread the bill over the year.

MAINTENANCE PAYMENTS
These are normally payable weekly through the courts. Turn to pp. 94–5 and 144–5 for more detailed consideration of maintenance.

FINES
If you have been fined by either the magistrates or Crown court, this will have to be included in your list of essential outgoings. Payments are normally weekly into court. It is important to pay, otherwise you may go to prison. If you find the weekly instalments difficult to manage on your income, the court has the power to reduce them, although it is difficult to get the total amount of the fine reduced without appealing to a higher court. For further details on how to reduce your fine repayments, see pp. 142–4.

It may take some time to organise a reduction in some Category 1 expenditure such as fines or maintenance payments, so for the time being include the full amount in your Financial Statement; if later on reductions do occur, that will give more flexibility in your budget and may enable you to pay more to creditors than originally agreed.

☞ You should now compare your Category 1 expenditure with your income (see Self-Help Kit, pp. 4 and 5). In most cases income will exceed expenditure and you can go on to look at your Category 2 costs. However, if at *this* stage you are spending more than your income, you are in very great difficulty. You will have to look again at maximising your income (Chapter 5); if you are on benefit, turn to the last section of this Chapter (p. 119).

If you are *self-employed*, this means that your business is not producing sufficient income to meet your basic essentials. You should consider whether you might be better off claiming benefits and ceasing to be self-employed. Some very drastic reductions in your spending may also have to be contemplated.

The Andersons

The Andersons' Category 1 expenditure works out as follows:

Mortgage	20.80
Rates	3.70
Water rates	1.92
Life insurance	2.00
House contents insurance	2.50
Electricity	10.00
Gas	5.40
Housekeeping	67.00
School meals	6.00
Pocket money	1.50
Travelling expenses	8.10
TV licence	1.25
	£130.17

Income	180.93
Less Category 1 outgoings	130.17
Balance	£50.76

John and Wendy are thus well within their income on Category 1 expenditure. Expenditure on life insurance is reasonable and the family does not run a car. John uses public transport to get to work, Christopher walks to school, and Sarah has a bus pass, which reduces her expenditure on travel. However, John and Wendy decide that in future they will use the 'pay-as-you-go' schemes for gas and electricity charges to spread the bills more evenly over the year. John and Wendy can now move on to look at their Category 2 outgoings.

Category 2 – Essential Items Difficult to Quantify

The main items in this section are likely to be:

- clothing/shoes

- school expenses

- books and toys for children

- repairs to property

- replacement of and repairs to essential household items

- redecoration

- health expenses (prescriptions, dental treatment, etc.)

- entertainment, birthdays, Christmas.

Category 2 expenditure will appear under two headings in your financial statement – 'Clothing and Miscellaneous'.

Clothing
Everyone needs shoes and clothing but it is extremely difficult to provide guidelines for reasonable expenditure. What is reasonable depends on many factors, such as age and size of family members, whether smart clothes are needed for work, or whether a uniform is provided, whether a family member is particularly hard on clothes or shoes due to disability. We hesitate to suggest any figure but our experience leads us to

believe that the absolute *minimum* figure to allow is £2 per person per week. If your children have to wear school uniform, you should include the cost of kitting them out in your figure for clothing and shoes. Calculate your clothing figure as the Andersons did in Chapter 4 (p. 68) and then consider whether you can justify that level of expenditure to any creditors who may query it.

Most people prefer to purchase new clothing for themselves and their family. However, bargains can sometimes be found at second-hand clothes shops, and charity shops.

Repairs and replacements
Future expenditure on these items is difficult to predict. Look at what you have spent over the last twelve months and use that figure to make an assessment for the future.

If you do need work doing to the house, always check your house insurance policy to see if the work in question is covered by the policy.

School expenses
School trips, photographs, parties, extra-curricula activities, and so on are very important to children. Make an allowance of approximately 50p per child per week for these, unless you can place a more accurate figure based on the actual cost of a particular activity (e.g. music lessons).

Health expenses
Unless you qualify for free prescriptions, dental treatment, spectacles, etc., these are items that must be planned for in your budget. We suggest that you allow £1 per week.

Entertainment, birthdays, Christmas, toys and books
Expenditure on these items may be more difficult to

justify, but most creditors recognise that some expenditure here is reasonable. The question is, how much? 'Entertainment' can cover the occasional evening out at the cinema or spending every evening at the pub – there is a world of difference in cost. Your expenditure on these items may have to be severely reduced to enable you to make realistic proposals to your creditors. However, some people are deeply committed to their leisure spending, and see it as a priority they will not surrender.

Budgeting for Category 2

Category 2 expenditure is principally irregular capital, or lump-sum spending, with the exception of entertainment. The temptation on a tight budget is to spend this money and not put it on one side for when it is required. We suggest therefore that you attempt to save a weekly amount as an aid to budgeting for these items. By putting the money into a deposit account, building society account or national savings account, not only will it be safe until you need it, but it will also earn some interest for you.

☞ Now add your Category 2 expenditure into your Financial Statement and compare your total essential outgoings with your income (see pp. 4 and 6 of Self-Help Kit). If your outgoings exceed income, look again at Category 1 and 2 expenditure and consider where economies could be made. Refer to Chapter 5 and, if living on benefit, the last section of this chapter.

The Andersons

Neither John or Wendy had to wear smart clothes for work, and Christopher does not have to wear a school uniform. At Sarah's school there is a uniform but John and Wendy have been able to buy most of it second-hand from a girl further up the school. They allow £11 per week for clothing. They cut Christmas and birthdays to £3 per week and will concentrate that money on the children. Entertainment is halved to £5 per week, and they continue to allow £1 for health and £1 for extra school expenses. They decide that they can cut expenditure on redecoration by doing the work themselves. They discover that the work to the drains is covered by their house insurance. Expenditure allowed for repairs and replacements is thus cut to £4 per week. Sarah has started piano lessons which cost £3 per week. They decide to continue these for the time being. They also have John's occasional overtime, which they may be able to use as an additional buffer against unexpected expense.

Their Category 2 expenditure thus works out as follows:

Clothing	11.00	
Miscellaneous	17.00	
	£28.00	

Income		180.93
Less Category 1	130.17	
Category 2	28.00	
		158.17
Balance		£22.76

John and Wendy can now move on to consider their Category 3 expenditure.

Category 3 – The Extras that Make Life Worthwhile

Into this category come items that are not essential to keep body and soul together. They present special problems when you are in financial difficulties and you may have to make some hard decisions about what is a necessity and what is not.

Expenditure that you may have to consider in this section is:

- cigarettes

- alcohol

- gambling/bingo

- holidays

- video rental

- meals out

- subscriptions to clubs

- sporting activities

- telephone

- hobbies

Cigarettes, alcohol, gambling
In small quantities, expenditure on these items may rank as entertainment, but in extreme cases of heavy smoking, drinking and gambling there is the question of addiction.

A packet of twenty cigarettes per day costs approximately £10.50 per week. To a creditor, such expenditure is inesssential. Cigarettes may have to appear in your Financial Statement, but it may be difficult to win creditors' cooperation unless some real effort is being made to reduce consumption or give up altogether. However, it is one thing to recognise the need to stop, and quite another actually to do it. If you are 'addicted' to cigarettes, the last thing you are going to want to do is add the further stress of giving up smoking to your financial stress. In our experience, there has to be very strong motivation. In one case clients could see that the £25 per week they were spending on cigarettes was jeopardising their home. If only they could reduce expenditure on cigarettes, they could catch up on their mortgage and save their home. They reduced expenditure to £7 per week and are still trying to cut it further.

In cases of heavy drinking and gambling, there may be a serious addiction. Little can be achieved in such a case until the member of the household who is addicted is prepared to accept that he or she has a problem that needs treatment. Once treatment has commenced the position can be explained to creditors and there can be some hope of money being redirected from the addiction to the creditors.

Holidays

Holidays are certainly very important to many people and this is recognised by many charities that provide holidays for people who cannot afford them. But expenditure on even a modest family holiday can make a large hole in a family's budget. In a debt situation the benefits to the family of taking a holiday have to be weighed against the benefits of paying off debts. The holidays rarely win.

Video rental

Creditors tend to take the view that a video is a luxury item that should be sacrificed so that commitments to them can be paid. But if the video helps with an Open University course, or provides important entertainment and stimulation for a mentally handicapped child, it may become an essential expenditure. If there is a good reason for renting the video, this can be explained to creditors; if there is not, this item may have to be sacrificed.

Telephone

Creditors often ask how clients can afford to be on the telephone when they owe money. The answer is that for some people a telephone is essential. For the family with a severely asthmatic child, a telephone may be a life-line enabling them to call for medical help quickly when an asthma attack occurs. For the elderly person living alone, a telephone can be an essential means of communication. Sometimes it can be invaluable in enabling someone who is unemployed to make the right contacts quickly, and thus get back into work. If there is a good reason for retaining the telephone, this may need to be explained to creditors in order to gain their cooperation.

☞ Category 3 expenditure in particular has to be looked at in the light of your debts and your credit commitments (which are considered in Chapters 7 and 8). You need to compare this expenditure with the money you have left over after subtracting Category 1 and 2 expenditure from your income. Any balance after deducting all your outgoings is your 'disposable income' that is available to allocate to your debts (see the Self-Help Kit, p. 7). If your total outgoings exceed your income, you will have to consider ways of making economies to free money for your debts.

The Andersons
John and Wendy have the following Category 3 expenditure on a weekly basis:

Holidays	3.95	
Newspapers	1.40	
Telephone	3.00	
Video rental	3.00	
	£11.35	

Income		180.93
Less Category 1	130.17	
Category 2	28.00	
Category 3	11.35	
		169.52
Balance (disposable income)		£11.41

As we saw in Chapter 4, the Andersons have minimum credit commitments of £20.60 per week; they have an electricity bill coming in three weeks' time that they cannot pay; they have mortgage arrears of £270.00; and they expect a rates bill in two months' time.

They decide that for the time being they must do without all Category 3 expenditure, although the holiday is the last thing they would wish to sacrifice. However, they feel that if John can obtain some further overtime during the next few months, they might be able to take a holiday later on. They cancel the newspapers, terminate the video rental, and ask Telecom to remove the telephone.

That leaves them with £22.76 per week to allocate to their debts. Things are starting to look a little better.

If your Category 1, 2 and 3 expenditure exceeds income, consider ways of making economies as the Andersons did to free money for paying your debts.

Category 4 – Credit Commitments

Where there are financial difficulties, weekly or monthly payments need to be reconsidered in the light of the total amount owed and of arrears that may exist in other areas of expenditure. These will be looked at in more detail in Chapters 7 and 8 when we consider how to renegotiate payments on debts.

Living on Benefit

If you are attempting to live on state benefit you may have found some of the above somewhat irrelevant. Claimants, particularly those on Supplementary Benefit, are usually living on or below the poverty line. When they have paid for housing, food and fuel, there is no money left over for anything else, so they are often forced into debt.

If John and Wendy Anderson both became unemployed and had to rely on state benefits, they would have a total income for themselves, Sarah and Christopher of:

	84.57
Plus Mary's contribution	17.50
David's contribution	20.00
Total income	£122.07

We know that their expenditure on basic essentials is £130.17, so they are already over £8 short if they have to rely on state benefits.

The family will have to look at both Category 1 and 2 expenditure and see where they can cut down. John's expenditure on travel may be reduced, but he still has expenses hunting for another job. Since they are only receiving the interest portion of their mortgage repayments from the DHSS, they will need to ask the building society to accept an 'interest only' payment for the time being, which will reduce their Category 1 expenditure.

Category 3 expenditure is usually unavailable to claimants, because if they cannot afford the basic essentials they certainly cannot afford the 'extras'.

There is no money left over for debts and credit commitments, which poses real problems for claimants in negotiating with creditors. However, it is still worth preparing a basic Financial Statement to show your actual income on benefit and how you are apportioning it between your various commitments, and to establish for creditors the dire financial position in which you find yourself. After all, such a situation is a problem for the creditor as well.

Your basic Financial Statement will at best show you how much money you have to deal with your debts – your 'disposable income'. At worst it will show you have no leeway at all. Either way, you now have your main tool for coping with your financial problems.

7

Priority Debts

Your Financial Statement has so far ignored your debts. These will be:

* arrears on continuing commitments – e.g. missed mortgage payments, rent arrears and unpaid fuel bills;

* the amounts you owe on loans and credit agreements;

* what you owe to friends and relatives.

This chapter is to help you decide which are your priority debts and look at strategies for dealing with them.

Two Vital Points

☞ The **Financial Statement** that we prepared in the last two chapters is your most important tool in your battle to get your affairs in order. It tells you how much money you have left with which to negotiate with your creditors. Make sure you have several copies, that it is as accurate as you can make it, and update it if your circumstances change.

☞ **Keep your creditors informed.** As far as a creditor is concerned, no news is *bad* news. Your Financial State-

ment can be the most important way of keeping
creditors informed, but even just answering letters and
explaining the reasons for your difficulty and how you
hope to work things out will win you time to consider
your position fully. Even if a creditor is rude or difficult,
do not give up, keep him informed.

When you have negotiated an agreement with a
creditor, you must keep to it. If you cannot, owing to a
change in circumstances, you must tell the creditor
what has happened, so that his confidence in your
integrity is maintained and an amended arrangement
can be made.

Listing Your Debts

The first thing to find out is exactly how much you owe.
You must list all arrears, loans and credit commitments.
If a further payment is due on a debt very soon and you
do not think that you will be able to pay it before you
have reached agreement with your creditors, then add
that payment into your debts. For example:

Lisa and Martin Evans have the following debts:

Mortgage arrears – building society	748.00
Rates due and unpaid	143.00
Electricity – red bill received	99.00
Clothing club – total outstanding	60.00
Loan from Martin's employer – total outstanding	120.00
Credit card – total outstanding	240.00
Total	£1,410.00

So Lisa and Martin appear to have total debts of
£1,410. However, the next month's mortgage payment of £216 is due and they may miss it. So they
are best advised to list the mortgage arrears as
£748 + £216 making total debts of £1,626.00.

This constitutes your schedule of debts.

Choosing Your Priorities

Some debts can result in more severe penalties for you than others. The worst consequences you can suffer are *loss of your home, loss of your fuel supply, distraint* (goods being removed from your home by bailiffs), and *imprisonment*. The debts where these situations could arise if you left things too long are:

Debt	Final sanctions
● Mortgage arrears	Repossession/Eviction
● Second mortgage/ secured loan arrears	Repossession/Eviction
● Rent arrears	Distraint/Eviction
● General rates arrears	Distraint/Imprisonment
● Water rates arrears	Disconnection
● Gas and electricity arrears	Disconnection
● Unpaid fines	Imprisonment
● Maintenance arrears	Imprisonment
● Income tax arrears	Distraint/Imprisonment
● VAT arrears	Distraint
● Hire purchase arrears (less than one-third paid)	Repossession without court proceedings

Most of these ultimate sanctions occur only after lengthy procedures or court proceedings; however, debts with so much at stake must be priorities.

Mortgage arrears
A mortgage is the legal term used to describe the pledging of property as security for a debt. The mortgage-granter is known legally as the mortgagee, the borrower as the mortgagor. The commonest form of mortgage is for house purchase. This will be a first mortgage and will take precedence over any later mortgage or secured loan taken out, for example, to do repairs or home improvements.

A first mortgage may be granted by a building

society, a local authority or a bank. A second mortgage, while it can be granted by a bank, is usually granted by a finance company or money lender. The mortgage deed, or contract, sets out the terms and conditions of the mortgage including the monthly repayment terms. With a first mortgage the repayments will normally be spread over 15–25 years at a low rate of interest. With a second mortgage, the rates of interest are usually higher and the mortgage term is much shorter – anything between two and ten years. The monthly repayments are thus proportionately greater.

In most cases the mortgage does not cover the full value of the property on the open market. The difference in value is called 'the equity'. This is calculated as follows:

Value of house if sold		30,000
First mortgage	18,000	
Second mortgage	4,000	
	£22,000	22,000
	Equity =	£8,000

The amount of equity you have in your house can be very important in deciding what to do if you get into arrears.

If you have first or second mortgage arrears , or both, the lender will write to you once or several times before commencing court proceedings for possession. The sooner you start negotiating the better, but first you need to gather together some information:

* how much the arrears amount to on both a first and, if you have one, a second mortgage;

* how much is outstanding on the total mortgage;

* whether your MIRAS figure has been correctly calculated;

* whether, on a first mortgage, switching from an endowment mortgage to a simple capital/interest one can reduce your monthly repayments AND produce a lump sum if you cash in the endowment policy;

* in the case of a second mortgage, the redemption figure for early settlement;

* in the case of a second mortgage, whether you should be, and are getting, tax relief on your monthly payments;

* how much your house is worth (you can ask an estate agent to value for sale without obligation);

* if you are in receipt of Supplementary Benefit, whether you are entitled to more help with both first and second mortgage repayments, and whether any claim can be backdated.

* whether your ongoing mortgage repayments have been properly calculated and incorporated in your financial statement.

PAYMENT ARRANGEMENTS
When you have this information you can consider the following strategies, and decide which is the most applicable to your situation.

Additional monthly payment
You offer an additional monthly payment to clear the arrears. The lender will normally ask for the arrears to be cleared over 12–18 months. Longer periods have been negotiated where the equity in the property is large, or where there are exceptional circumstances, such as prolonged illness, death of a partner, or marital breakdown.

Interest-only payments
If you are on Supplementary Benefit, in receipt of Family Income Supplement or otherwise on a low in-

come, it may be possible to persuade your lender to accept an 'interest only' payment off the mortgage, plus a nominal amount off the arrears. This would have to be negotiated as a temporary arrangement whilst you try to improve your income. A lender would not be willing to agree to this as a permanent arrangement, and will be reluctant if there are already substantial arrears.

No payment
In exceptional circumstances a lender may be prepared to suspend monthly payments for a short period, usually not longer than three months, if satisfied that at the end of that period money will be forthcoming by way of a lump-sum payment or substantial additional monthly payments.

Capitalisation of arrears
This is normally available only in the case of first mortgage arrears and where there is a substantial equity in the property. The first mortgage is increased to include the arrears and the monthly repayments are increased to take account of this. The arrears are thus spread over the remaining mortgage term. For example:

> Kate and Philip Brown have a mortgage of £12,000 on a house worth £25,000. Philip has been unemployed for nine months and there are mortgage arrears of £730. He now has work again, but cannot afford to offer an additional monthly payment to clear the arrears over 12 months. He asks the lender to capitalise the arrears by increasing his mortgage to £12,730 (plus costs of drawing up new deeds), and thus spreads his arrears and costs over the remaining mortgage term – in his case 18 years.

A lender is more likely to agree to this strategy if you can provide some evidence of the worth of your property, such as details of what similar properties in the area have sold for recently.

Remortgage

If your original lender is not prepared to negotiate with you or discuss the possible strategies, another may be prepared to grant a new mortgage on your property to pay off the original mortgage and arrears. This is particularly useful if you have arrears on a second mortgage, and the lender is threatening to take court proceedings to take possession of your home. The first mortgage company may be prepared to help you, or a new mortgage could pay off both first and second mortgages, plus arrears, and leave you with only one monthly payment to a new lender.

For example:

> June and Kenneth Black had a first mortgage with the local authority for £6,000, on which the monthly payments were £56 (with tax relief). They took out a second mortgage to have double-glazing fitted. The double glazing cost £4,500, but with interest the loan was £9,630 spread over 10 years with monthly payments of £80. They got behind with the second mortgage and the company demanded £125 per month to clear the arrears. June and Kenneth could not pay, so they remortgaged the property (worth £18,000) with a reputable building society. £6,000 went to the local authority to pay off the first mortgage, and the redemption figure on the second mortgage for early settlement was £6,800, so with costs their new mortgage was £13,000. Instead of having to pay £181 per month to two mortgagees they had one mortgage repayment of £126 per month.

Only accept a remortgage offer from a reputable lender such as a building society, and make sure that you can afford the new monthly payments before going ahead.

Local authority buy-back

If you have purchased a council house and find you

cannot manage your mortgage repayments, you should consider enquiring whether your local authority Mortgage Department would repurchase the property, and, if so, whether they would allow you to continue living there as a tenant.

Sale

If your arrears are large and all other strategies have failed, the sale of your house may be the inevitable option.

Not only will this be emotionally very difficult for you, but there may be problems obtaining suitable rehousing. However, if all else fails you must consider selling. It is better for you to sell the property yourself rather than wait for a court order for eviction, by the mortgagee. If you sell yourself you have control over the selling price, somewhere to live whilst the sale takes place and the chance to show prospective buyers the house whilst it is furnished and occupied, and thus more attractive.

Once you have put the house on the market you must consider where you and your family will live after the sale. If the equity remaining cannot buy another smaller house that you can afford to run, you will have to consider renting. The Housing (Homeless Persons) Act 1977 places obligations on the local authority Housing Department to rehouse homeless persons in certain circumstances, if they have a 'priority need'. Contact the Housing Department and see if they will rehouse you. A more attractive alternative may be to rent a property from a housing association. Contact your Housing Aid Centre or Citizens' Advice Bureau for more information and a list of housing associations in the area.

Abandoning the property

If you have failed to sell the house, it may be tempting to hand the keys back to the lender, or just to abandon the property, leaving the lender to sell it.

Do not do this during the months when the house is empty, prior to resale, the mortgage instalments will carry on accumulating and eating into any equity. The lender will have to pay an estate agent to show prospective purchasers around, and these costs will also eat into the equity. The property will be more difficult to sell empty and unfurnished, and is liable to become vandalised, thus diminishing the value further.

Try and stay put and sell the property yourself, even if it means reducing the asking price.

Borrowing
Borrowing to pay off debts is a risky business (see Chapter 4, pp. 72–3). Do not resort to this strategy until you have carefully considered the other options and the points set out in Chapter 4.

SECOND MORTGAGES – SPECIAL PROBLEMS
Because they come second in line, companies offering secured loans or second mortgages are generally less tolerant of arrears than first mortgage companies. At the worst, some second mortgage companies will resort to court action as soon as arrears occur. This attitude makes negotiating difficult. If you are involved with a lender like this, try negotiating, but if that fails it may be worth letting matters go to a first court hearing. You may get a better deal from the court than the lender is offering. See Chapter 9 for further consideration of court proceedings.

GENERAL POINTS ABOUT MORTGAGE ARREARS
The strategies above are all best tried as soon as possible and are most successful when used *before* the first court hearing. But even if your lender has started court proceedings or there has been a hearing, you should still keep in touch and try to negotiate.

When you are ready to suggest possible strategies for dealing with your mortgage arrears, make an appointment to see the most senior person that you can, since our experience is that the higher you go in an organisation the more considerate the treatment you will receive. Remember that the counter clerk at the building society's local office may not have the authority to make decisions on the sort of strategies that you are considering.

If you feel that the offer you have made to the lender is reasonable in all the circumstances, and has nevertheless been refused, consider writing to the head office of the building society – explain your financial position, send a copy of your Financial Statement, explain the offer you have made, and ask for advice. If you are successful in your negotiations and a verbal agreement has been arrived at with your mortgage-granter, confirm the agreement in writing and keep copies of all your letters, and any replies.

Rent arrears
If you have rent arrears, your landlord will probably have already written to you or visited to discuss the problem.

Remember!
He cannot evict you from the property without going to court and getting a court order. If he harasses you to try and get you to leave without doing this, he is committing an offence (see Chapter 3, p. 58).

THINGS YOU NEED TO CHECK
* *Housing Benefit.* If you are having difficulty paying your rent and are unemployed or on a pension, you may be entitled to Housing Benefit in the form of a rent rebate or rent allowance (see Chapter 5, p. 86). The Housing Department can backdate benefit for up to 12 months if they are satisfied that there are exceptional circumstances. Inform your landlord if you qualify, and explain that it may take a while for the department to calculate your benefit.

* *Fair rent registration.* If you are living in privately rented accommodation and think you are paying too much, you can apply to the Rent Officer to have a fair rent registered on your home. The Rent Officer will visit your property, assess it and compare the rent with other similar properties in the area, and decide what the rent should be. He may increase or decrease it. Once a fair rent is registered, your landlord cannot

charge you more unless he re-applies to the Rent Officer.

Application forms and more information can be obtained from the Rent Officer (in the telephone directory under 'Rent Officer Service').

PAYMENT ARRANGEMENTS

If you are a tenant you are in quite a good negotiating position, since your landlord will be reluctant to start court proceedings, which are costly and time consuming.

Additional weekly payment

Visit or write to your landlord and offer a weekly amount from the money you have available for debts to clear the arrears. If your income is low, your landlord should be prepared to accept a small amount, maybe £1 each week, until the arrears are paid off. If your income is high or your disposable income is substantial, your landlord will expect you to offer more. Use your Financial Statement to justify your offer. If your landlord is the local authority or a housing association, they will prefer a small regular amount rather than the promise of a larger amount that never materialises. Private landlords may prefer to go to court.

Rent direct

If you are in receipt of Housing Benefit/rent allowance, you may be allowed to arrange to have this paid directly to your landlord by the Housing Department. This can help to prevent further rent arrears accruing.

If you are in receipt of 100 per cent certificated Housing Benefit because you claim Supplementary Benefit, you can arrange for a rent arrears payment to be deducted from your basic benefit and paid to your landlord directly by the DHSS. Whether this facility will survive the social security reforms is unknown.

DISTRAINT

Landlords cannot take possession of your property without a court order, but they do have another sanction when rent arrears have accrued. Distraint entitles the landlord to instruct a private bailiff to visit your home and take possession of your belongings until you have paid the rent arrears. If you do not pay within a set period of time, normally seven days, the bailiff can then arrange to sell your belongings through an auction house. The proceeds of the sale go to pay the auctioneer's costs, the bailiff's costs and the landlord to meet the arrears.

In practice, very few landlords use this sanction and only as a last resort. Some local authorities and housing associations have taken a policy decision not to use distraint. However, if you fail to contact your landlord and explain your position, he may take the view that you are irresponsible and distrain to attempt to make you pay.

If you have already received a bailiff's visit or one is threatened, it is essential to contact the bailiff's office and your landlord at once and make an offer of payment, using your Financial Statement to justify your offer. Once the bailiffs have removed your belongings, only a substantial offer to pay off the arrears quickly will prevent the sale taking place.

Rates arrears

There are two very powerful sanctions attached to non-payment of rates: distraint and imprisonment. The way rates are calculated is presently under review by the government, but it seems unlikely that this would lead to a change in the need to give priority to this outgoing.

THE LOCAL AUTHORITY'S PROCEDURE

Rates payment and arrears are normally dealt with by the Borough, City or County Treasurer's Department of your local authority. The procedures they usually follow in pursuing rates payments are as follows:

---

(1) First demand for six months' rates in advance, in April and October.
    OR First demand for combined twelve months' rates.
(2) Second demand for six months' rates in advance.

(3)   Magistrates' court summons for non-payment of rates.

(4)   If no offer of payment or appearance at magistrates' court, magistrates will issue distraint warrant.

(5)   Bailiffs attend at your home to execute distraint warrant. They remove your goods and sell them at auction.

(6)   If distraint does not produce all of the money owed, further magistrates' courts proceedings will take place. A 'show cause' warrant will be issued for your attendance at court to explain non-payment of the rates.

(7)   Magistrate likely to impose order of committal to prison, suspended on payment of £x per week off arrears.

(8)   If further default, imprisonment will follow.

The first action to take in all cases is to check with your local authority whether you are entitled to a *rate rebate* through the Housing Benefit scheme. A backdated rate rebate could wipe out your arrears and cut your rate commitments for the future.

PAYMENT ARRANGEMENTS

The action you take in dealing with your rate arrears will depend on which stage in the enforcement procedure your case has reached. Whatever stage your case has reached, you should contact the Rates Department and explain your financial situation to them, using your Financial Statement.

If enforcement procedures are between stages (1) and (3) above, contact the Rates Department and offer a weekly sum from your disposable income, to enable you to clear the arrears prior to the next six-monthly bill. For example, if, on 1 July, £120 is outstanding on your April bill, you will need to offer £120 ÷ 13 = £9.23 (i.e. £9.25) per week to clear the arrears before the next bill arrives in October. If you cannot afford to pay enough to clear the arrears, offer less, and justify your position with your Financial Statement.

If proceedings have reached stage (3), you should attend the magistrates' court hearing with a copy of your Financial Statement and a schedule of all your other debts and make an offer of payment off the arrears. You should be able to justify this offer by presenting to the magistrates your Financial Statement.

If enforcement procedure is between stages (4) and (6), the matter will now be in the hands of a private certificated bailiff. Contact the bailiff, with whom it is likely to be difficult to negotiate, and attempt to arrange a weekly payment to clear the arrears so that the bailiff holds the distraint warrant and does not need to visit your house and remove your goods and sell them.

If the enforcement procedure has reached stage (5) and your goods have already been removed and sold, that unfortunately is not the end of the matter. You should contact the Rates Department and find out whether the sale of your goods has cleared the debt. If it has not, you will be required to make a further appearance before the magistrates. If no 'show cause' warrant has been issued, it may be possible for you to arrange to appear at a time convenient to yourself. If a 'show cause' warrant has already been issued, you will have to attend at the time appointed by the magistrates. When you go to court you should present a Financial Statement and a schedule of your other debts, and make an offer of repayment of the arrears.

If stage (7) has been reached and you find you cannot make the payments ordered, as a result of a change in your circumstances, contact the Rates Department and the magistrates' Clerk's Office, explain your position and ask for another hearing for the instalments to be reconsidered.

If stage (8) has been reached and the magistrates have already imposed a sentence of imprisonment suspended on payment of the arrears and you have defaulted on that agreement, then unfortunately only

payment in full of the arrears is likely to prevent
imprisonment.

The sentence of imprisonment which you serve will
depend on how much you owe. It does not wipe out the
arrears but is a punishment for non-payment. However
in practice after your release it is likely that the arrears
will be 'remitted' or written off.

THE FUTURE
It is sensible after resolving your arrears problem to ask
the Rates Department if you can pay monthly, so that
you avoid rates arrears in future. Most local authorities
accept monthly payments and some issue a payment
book to help you keep a proper record.

Water rates arrears
The ultimate sanction for water rates arrears is disconnection of your water supply. Most water authorities
use this sanction only as a last resort and most reluctantly, because of the health risks to consumers and
their families if the water supply is disconnected.

Payment of water rates is normally half-yearly, but if
you are experiencing difficulty paying these bills you
should ask to pay by monthly instalments and request a
payment book.

If you have an unpaid bill you should negotiate with
the water authority, showing them a copy of your
Financial Statement. They will probably require
advance payment of your arrears, which will enable
you to spread the arrears over the remaining weeks
until the arrival of the next bill.

If you fail to contact your water board and fail to
negotiate with them, they will probably sue you in the
county court for the outstanding amount. It is unwise
to let matters proceed to this stage since costs are
incurred once court proceedings have been commenced.

If you are in receipt of a default summons concerning
water rates, you need to make an offer to the water
authority through the courts on the form which has

been sent to you. If you have lost the form you can get
another one from the county court office.

More details on county court procedure are given in
Chapter 9.

═══

Fuel debts
The sanction for fuel debt is disconnection. It is essential to *take action quickly*, since the fuel boards can move
to disconnection in a matter of *two or three weeks*. No
court or independent assessor is involved in the
decision. Once disconnected, it can be very difficult to
get your supply reconnected. You will normally be
asked to pay a substantial deposit on top of clearing the
outstanding debt and paying a reconnection charge.

The fuel board is all powerful but, as a result of
increasingly higher rates of disconnection, a 'Code of
Practice' on disconnection was issued in the late 1970s
to which the fuel boards should adhere. Unfortunately
the Code gives only limited protection.

CODE OF PRACTICE
You should get a copy from your local gas or electricity
office if you have a fuel debt. The Code is basically there
to protect consumers who fall into the hardship categories, which are:

* consumers in receipt of Supplementary Benefit, Unemployment Benefit or Family Income Supplement;

* old age pensioners;

* the blind, the sick or disabled;

* consumers with children under 11 years of age.

If you fall into the hardship categories, the Code of
Practice states that the fuel board should not disconnect
you until either social security (the DHSS) or the social
services (Local Authority social workers) have been
contacted about your case. If you tell the fuel board you
are contacting either the DHSS or social services, the

fuel board should hold your disconnection for at least
14 days, so that these agencies can see if they can help
you. It is therefore worth checking with them to see
what they can do.

If social services and/or DHSS cannot help you, then
the fuel boards can disconnect unless you make some
arrangements with them to pay off the bill. The only
people who are given further protection by the Code of
Practice are consumers in receipt of old age pensions,
who in certain circumstances will not be disconnected
during the winter months of October to March.

If you have any complaints about the way the fuel
board has treated you or operates in general you should
report this to, in the case of electricity, your local
Electricity Consultative Council, and in the case of gas,
to the Gas Consumers' Council. However, it has been
our experience that, unless there has been a breach of
the Code of Practice, these two organisations are unlikely to provide you with a great deal of satisfaction.

If you have a genuine grievance against your local
fuel board, you are more likely to get results by
complaining to your local councillor or Member of
Parliament, or by writing to the local newspaper.

PAYMENT ARRANGEMENTS

Payment prior to next quarterly bill
The fuel board ask for the outstanding quarterly bill to
be cleared in instalments before the date on which the
next quarterly bill is due to arrive. For example:

Mr and Mrs Peters owe the electricity board £135.
They have received a first bill, a second demand
and a disconnection notice. They contact the fuel
board to explain they cannot pay. They are invited
to pay by instalments prior to the next bill. The
next quarterly account is due in seven weeks' time
and therefore they are asked to pay by instalments
of £18.20 per week.

Advantages:

* The only advantage of this method of payment is that it is quickly agreed and negotiated with the fuel board and is the payment arrangement that the fuel boards themselves tend to offer as a solution.

Disadvantages:

* This payment arrangement envisages that you will carry on paying for your fuel by a quarterly account in the future. This is bad financial management if you are on a tight budget. What you probably need to do is to make arrangements to pay small amounts regularly rather than large amounts irregularly.

* No money is being saved towards the next quarterly bill, so exactly the same problem will occur when that bill falls due.

* Due to the dwindling amount of time available to pay the bill, instalments demanded are often very large (as in the case of the above example) and it may be impossible to pay in the time given.

Slot meter

Most fuel boards are prepared to install a slot or pre-payment meter as a method of dealing with a fuel debt, but only if it is safe and practical. Fuel boards will usually refuse a slot meter in areas where there are high rates of burglary or where it is necessary to move the meter because this is costly.

If a slot meter is fitted the debt will be collected by calibrating the meter up, sometimes by as much as 60 per cent. The cost of fitting the meter may also be recovered by calibration. For example:

Mr and Mrs Peters owe the fuel board £135. They apply to have a slot meter fitted, for which the fuel board quote £70. Mr and Mrs Peters cannot afford

£70 so the slot meter is calibrated to clear not only the arrears but also the fitting costs. £135 + £70 = £205. If Mr and Mrs Peters consume on average £10 of electricity a week, this may now cost them £16 per week, and it will take 35 weeks to clear the arrears.

Advantages:

* This is the ultimate 'pay-as-you-go' scheme. With this method it should be impossible to get into further debt, unless you suffer a meter theft.

Disadvantages:

* If your slot meter is burgled you will normally be expected by the fuel board to repay the stolen money, irrespective of who committed the theft. Some fuel boards are prepared to waive this rule if you can establish that a genuine burglary has taken place. You may need the assistance of the police in establishing that a genuine break-in has occurred, since it is the view of fuel boards that most meter thefts are by the customers themselves.

* The cost of installing a slot meter, particularly if it is necessary to move the meter from outside the property, can be as much as £200. This installation fee has to be paid by the consumer. If you are in receipt of Supplementary Benefit it may be possible to persuade the DHSS to make a single payment to cover the installation fee (until such time as single payments are abolished under proposed legislation).

* The fuel board decides on the calibration of the slot meter, but it should be reasonable and take into account your financial circumstances. However, it is likely that, the greater the arrears, the higher the amount of money you will have to feed into the meter to maintain your electricity supply.

* Budgeting is difficult because you will need to put more money in the meter in the winter than in the summer.

* Slot meter payment is unsuitable for some forms of central heating.

* Both gas and electricity when supplied through a slot meter are marginally more expensive than when paid for on a budget scheme or quarterly account.

Token meters
Some fuel boards are now experimenting with token meters, which are operated by tokens purchased from the fuel board or the local Post Office. The advantage of these meters is that there is nothing to be gained in breaking into one since the value of the token is cancelled as soon as it is pushed into the meter.

Budget scheme
With this payment arrangement the fuel board calculates your average weekly or monthly consumption figure and then adds on the arrears spread over a period of time, which may be as much as 18 months. For example:

> Mr and Mrs Peters owe £135 to the electricity board. Consumption of electricity over a year works out at £135 per winter quarter and £85 per summer quarter; £440 per annum divided by 52 = £8.46 per week. Therefore the weekly budget for ongoing consumption is £9 per week. Arrears of £135 divided by 52 = £2.59. The total weekly payment becomes £11.60 until the arrears are paid off, and £9 thereafter.

Advantages:

* This is likely to be the cheapest way of coping with current consumption, and also paying off a fuel debt.

* If weekly payments can be arranged, this is a great aid to budgeting.

* Payments are spread evenly over the year rather than being greater in the winter than in the summer.

Disadvantages:

* Those on a very tight budget, e.g. claimants, may find it difficult to adhere to a weekly or monthly budget scheme and missing even one payment can be disastrous.

* Once onto a budget scheme, consumption often increases. This then requires a reappraisal by the fuel board of their weekly or monthly figures.

* Some fuel boards will not allow consumers onto a budget scheme until any arrears have been paid. In some areas, Mr and Mrs Peters would not have been eligible to go onto a budget scheme until they had actually paid the £135 they owed.

Fuel direct
Only consumers in receipt of Supplemetary Benefit can consider this option. When Supplementary Benefit is replaced by Income Support, it is unlikely that this facility will be open to claimants.

The DHSS withhold part of the benefit each week and pay it to the fuel board on behalf of the claimant. In return the fuel board agrees not to disconnect. The amount of the weekly deduction is usually calculated by adding together the ongoing estimated average weekly cost of the fuel used, plus a maximum (currently £2.95) towards the arrears. For example:

Mr and Mrs Peters are in receipt of Supplementary Benefit. They owe the electricity board £135. They cannot pay this amount out of their weekly benefit and therefore apply to the DHSS for a fuel direct payment. The DHSS contact the fuel board

> who inform them that the average consumption figure is £10 per week. The DHSS add on £2.95 per week off the arrears so that £12.95 per week is deducted from Mr and Mrs Peters' Supplementary Benefit and paid over to the fuel board.

Advantages:

* The direct payment scheme virtually guarantees that disconnection will not take place.

* Responsiblity for payment is taken away from the claimant, thus reducing the pressure on the claimant's budget.

* The arrears are collected at a set rate of a maximum of £2.95 per week, irrespective of the level of the debt. This figure is uprated periodically.

Disadvantages:

* Direct deduction from the claimant's Supplementary Benefit reduces the amount of income in the claimant's own hands.

* Claimants' consumption of fuel often goes up sharply when they move onto the direct payment scheme, causing the fuel board to apply for an increase in the direct payment, which further reduces the amount of money payable to the claimant for other essential outgoings.

Fines
Fines are normally imposed by the Crown court or magistrates' court, but enforced through the magistrates' court 'Fines and Fees' Department.

Normal procedure
The procedure that the local Fines and Fees Department will adopt is probably as follows, although there are local variations:

(1) Imposition of fine with instalment order or set time for payment in full, e.g. 14 days.

(2) In default of payments, warrant issued for defaulter to be arrested and brought before the courts to 'show cause' why he has not paid his instalments.

(3) 'Show cause' hearing where magistrates are likely to commmit to prison for a set period of time, suspended on payment of £x per week. If payment is made, the sentence of imprisonment will not have to be served.

(4) If further default occurs, magistrates issue a warrant committing the defaulter to prison.

(5) Defaulter is arrested and taken straight to prison to serve his sentence.

PAYMENT ARRANGEMENTS

You need to ascertain which stage your unpaid fines have reached by telephoning the courts. It is inadvisable to attend at court until you have done this, since this may render you liable to arrest, and/or imprisonment then and there.

If the enforcement procedure is still at stage (1) and you cannot afford the instalments, or want further time to pay, then attend at the magistrates' court and make an application for further time or a reduction in the instalment order. You should be given a hearing date. Take to the hearing your Financial Statement, a schedule of your debts and an offer of payment to make to the magistrates.

If stage (2) has been reached, find out from the magistrates' Clerk's Office the date when magistrates are next dealing with fines arrears. Attend at court at 9.30 in the morning with your Financial Statement, schedule of debts and an offer of payment.

If proceedings have reached stage (3) it is still possible to apply for a reduction in the instalments order.

If stage (4) has been reached, only payment of the arrears in full can prevent your arrest and imprisonment.

Once arrested and taken to prison, each day served will reduce the amount owed on the fine until the whole amount is wiped out and you are released. Payment of the outstanding amount can be made whilst a sentence is being served, so that release can be obtained immediately. For example:

> Fine £200. Sentence in default of payment – 20 days, i.e. £10 per day. After five days' imprisonment has been served, £50 is paid, and £150 will purchase immediate release.

Remember!
The magistrates' court is primarily a criminal court. You will be expected to stand up when you are spoken to by the magistrates or their clerks, and you will be expected to call the magistrate 'Sir' or 'Madam'. An appearance in a magistrates' court can be an intimidating experience. If you take along with you your Financial Statement and schedule of your other debts to hand in to the magistrates' Clerk at the beginning of your hearing, it will make the whole experience a lot easier both for yourself and the court. The hearing itself will normally take only a short time, and it is well worth putting up with a few minutes embarrassment or inconvenience if it will ultimately produce a good result.

Maintenance arrears
Maintenance orders for a former wife or husband, or for children, may be imposed by the High Court, a county court, or a magistrates' court, but are usually registered in the magistrates' court for enforcement.

If you have been ordered to pay maintenance and cannot afford the payments, as a result of either your income decreasing or your outgoings increasing, you should apply straight away for a variation of the order and should not wait for arrears to accrue. If arrears have already accrued, this does not prevent you from making an application for a variation. Consider consulting a legal aid solicitor for advice. The magistrates should then fix a hearing to deal with the case. You will need to take to the hearing your Financial Statement, schedule of debts and an offer of payment. If you leave the arrears to go on accruing, sooner or later you will be summoned to appear before the magistrates' court to explain why you have not paid, so it is sensible to make an application to the court prior to their issuing a summons for your attendance.

The magistrates also have the power to 'remit' the arrears. This in practice means that the arrears are wiped out. At any hearing for a variation of the maintenance order it is always worth asking the magistrates to remit the outstanding arrears. If the magistrates are not prepared to remit the arrears they will normally order you to pay an additional amount every week until the arrears are cleared.

For example:

> In January 1984 Bill Johnson was ordered to pay £10 per week maintenance for his wife and £5 per week maintenance for each of his three children. He paid that for two years but in January 1986 he remarried and took on additional commitments. By June 1986 there were maintenance arrears of £260. Bill was summoned before the magistrates' court and attended with a Financial Statement showing that he could only afford £18 per week. The magistrates agreed with him and reduced the maintenance for the wife to £2 per week, continued the order of £5 per week for each of the three children, and ordered him to pay £1 per week off the arrears – thus making an order of £18.

Hire purchase payments and arrears
Under normal circumstances we would not consider
hire purchase payments to be a priority, and would
deal with them alongside the other consumer credit
commitments (see Chapter 8). But hire purchase may
become a priority if a vital item is liable to be repossessed because payments cease or arrears have
accrued.

If you have entered into a hire purchase agreement,
you do not actually own the goods that are the subject
of the agreement until the very last instalment has been
paid to the credit-granter. If you default on any payment under the agreement, the credit-granter can repossess the goods. To give the hirer or purchaser a
measure of protection against 'snatch backs', legislation has been passed that states that where the hirer
has paid more than one-third of the purchase price over
to the credit-granter and then defaults there can be no
repossession of goods without the credit-granter first
applying for a court order.

Courts in practice are reluctant to order repossessions
where there is a possibility of the hirer continuing to
make some sort of payment to the credit-granter, so this
provides the hirer with a large measure of protection.
Many credit-granters will threaten repossession as a
lever to persuade defaulters to pay. However, this is not
a satisfactory solution because second-hand furniture
or electrical items have very little resale value. What the
credit-granter wants in these circumstances is the
opportunity to negotiate repayments that both sides
will find acceptable. You should attempt to negotiate
a reduction in payments but, if that fails, vital items
on hire purchase may have to be included in your
Financial Statement as essential outgoings. Refrigera-
tors, cookers, carpets, beds, and washing machines
would fall into this category. A family with three young
children all in nappies should not have any difficulty
persuading other creditors that a washing machine on
hire purchase was an essential item and that any
arrears on the hire purchase agreement were priority
debts.

Priority debts for the self-employed

If you are self-employed you may not have made
proper provision for your income tax, VAT or national
insurance contributions. Negotiating with the Inland
Revenue for unpaid tax, the Customs & Excise for
unpaid VAT and the DHSS for unpaid national insurance contributions is never easy. In our experience it
becomes easier when you have ceased trading. If you
owe substantial sums to these creditors, you need to
think very carefully about continuing to trade, and
perhaps seek the advice of a reputable chartered
accountant.

If you cannot afford to pay an accountant's fee, the
Small Business Advisory Service may be able to help
you. You can find the telephone number in your local
directory. In addition, some Citizens' Advice Bureaux
have accountants as volunteers who will give basic
advice to the self-employed on tax matters.

If you have ceased trading and are now employed or
on benefit, you should inform the Inland Revenue,
Customs & Excise and DHSS of this fact, send them a
Financial Statement showing income and outgoings,
come to an agreement with them on how much you
owe and make an offer to repay on weekly or monthly
terms from your disposable income – if you have any.

More Than One Priority Debt

It is quite possible that you will have more than one
priority debt to deal with, so you have to rationalise the
conflicting claims and sanctions of your priority
creditors.

The best practice is to begin with the priority debt
that is nearest to its final sanction. Negotiate with that
creditor first, and when you have reached agreement
move onto the priority debt that is second in line for
reaching its ultimate sanction. Each time you will have
to try to reserve some of your disposable income for the
remaining unresolved priority debts.

For example:

Lisa and Martin Evans have three priority debts –
mortgage arrears, rates arrears and an electricity
debt. They work out that they have a disposable
income of £25 per week.

They know that their most pressing debt is the
mortgage because the building society have
written to tell them that they will start court
proceedings in seven days. They make an
appointment to see their branch manager, taking
along their Financial Statement and a schedule of
their debts. The manager wants the arrears of £964
cleared in 12 months. This would cost Lisa and
Martin £20 per week. They believe they cannot
pay this because the rates will have to
be paid before the next bill is due, and they also
have to speak to the electricity board. They
explain this to the manager, and ask if the arrears
can be spread over 18 months. He reluctantly
agrees, making the stipulation that the current
mortgage of £216 per month plus £53 off the
arrears is paid by bankers' order.

Lisa and Martin then contact the Rates Department and offer £9 per week to clear their rates bill
of £143 in 16 weeks, just before the next bill falls
due. They have already allowed £5.50 per week in
their Financial Statement for rates, so now have to
find an additional £3.50 from their disposable
income.

They ask the electricity board if they can go
onto an easy-payments scheme. The board quote
a figure of £9.50 per week – £7.00 for ongoing
consumption and £2.50 off the arrears. Lisa and
Martin build the new payments into their
Financial Statement.

The arrears have thus used up £19.50 of their
disposable income, leaving £5.50 per week for
their remaining debts.

As you go through your priority debts and negotiate with each creditor, confirm your agreements in writing, keeping copies of all your letters and replies. You should then add these new payments into your Financial Statement (see Self-Help Kit, p. 8), so that your priority debts become part of your weekly or monthly expenditure. Any balance after including your priority debt payments is your 'final disposable income' that is available to allocate to your other debts.

Priority Debts – No Disposable Income

If at the end of your basic Financial Statement you have priority debts but no disposable income, you will have to go back and look again at your outgoings, to see whether you can cut expenditure somewhere to produce some money. It may mean you and the family going without new clothes for a period of time, or maybe cutting down on housekeeping. If this is your position, do not be frightened or too proud to tell your priority creditor. If they know that you are prepared to make such sacrifices to try to pay your debts, they will perhaps be prepared to treat you as a special case and accept smaller payments than they would normally demand.

You should also re-read Chapter 5 *and* make sure you are getting all the state benefits to which you are entitled.

Conclusion

The importance of paying priority debts first is to save your home, your warmth and, in some cases, your liberty. Priority creditors are not the people who knock on your door, or telephone you, asking for payment. They write and do not seem so pressing. It is important not to be misled by this seeming unconcern. They do not need to press you. They can secure payment by their sanctions.

Many people are worried by debt collectors knocking on the door or telephoning with demands for money. They are rarely pursuing priority debts. They do this to try and get in first. It is their way of competing with creditors who in reality have more powerful sanctions. Some of them will not care if you lose your home or electricity as long as they are paid first with what little money you have. Remember, if you give in to their pressure when you have unresolved priority debts, you will make things worse.

8

Unsecured Debts

The difference between priority debts and other debts is that other creditors' legal sanctions are not so drastic. Unsecured creditors cannot immediately threaten your home, fuel supply or your liberty; their remedy is to sue in the courts to recover the money that they have lent you. The court may sound frightening but it can be your friend too if:

* you can show you are really trying to pay your creditors but have had problems that have made things difficult;

* you can show the court, using your Financial Statement, how much money you have left to pay your debts.

We hope, however, that by taking the steps set out in this chapter you can reach agreement with your remaining creditors without it being necessary for them to resort to court action.

In this chapter we shall be looking at the debts of Debbie and Robert Hunt. They owe money to:

> Johnsons Clothing Catalogue
> Micawber Trust Finance Co. Ltd
> Flexible Bank Card plc
> Merchandise Credit Co. Ltd
> Easicheck Financial Services Ltd

The Facts You Need

Before dealing with your remaining debts you need the following information:

* copies of the credit agreements you signed when you first borrowed;

* the *total* amount you owe to each creditor, including any arrears;

* the rate of interest you are being charged and whether any extra charges are, or could be, added on to your account;

* whether your agreement is a revolving credit account, and if so how much is being charged in interest each month.

If you do not have the information available, you need to write to each creditor asking for it. This is the letter Robert Hunt wrote:

---

64 South Street,
Kitebridge,
Pentshire.

Dear Sir,

Re: Account No. 6263/H23/84

Please could you let me know as soon as possible the following information:

1. The *total* amount outstanding on the above account.
2. Whether any interest or service charges are presently being charged to this account, and if so how much per month.
3. Whether the account is a revolving credit account or a fixed-term credit agreement.

Please could you also send me a copy of the

> agreement which I signed when I first borrowed the money, since I have lost my copy.
>
> When I have this information I shall be in touch with you again in the near future.
>
> Yours faithfully,
>
> ROBERT HUNT

When creditors have replied to your letters and you have a full picture of your position, you need first to consider whether there is any legal remedy that may assist you. Ask yourself the following questions:

* *Has the creditor got a licence to grant credit under the Consumer Credit Act 1974?*

If he has not, and he has granted credit of more than £50, he has committed a criminal offence. In addition, he cannot enforce the agreement against the borrower unless he applies for, and is granted, permission by the Director General of Fair Trading. If you think the creditor is unlicensed, check with your local Trading Standards or Consumer Services Department.

* *Does the agreement contain the information required by the Consumer Credit Act 1974?*

Most credit agreements entered into *after* 19 May 1985 must be in the prescribed form, as set out in Chapter 2 (p. 40). If your agreement is dated after 19 May 1985 and does not seem to contain these items, then you may be able to challenge the creditor's right to enforce the debt against you; in any event he can only do so with the specific permission of the county court. Take some advice on the agreement and if it does infringe the requirements of the Act, you will be in a strong bargaining position with your creditor; by drawing the fact to the creditor's attention, the creditor may decide not to pursue the matter any further.

Here is a suggested letter to write to your creditor if this situation occurs:

Dear Sirs,

Re: Agreement No. 109 GH 170

On 10 June 1986 I entered into the above agreement with your company. I am now advised that the agreement does not comply with the requirements of the Consumer Credit Act 1974 due to the fact that the APR was omitted from the agreement.

In these circumstances I am told that the agreement cannot be enforced against me without an order of the court.

Plese could you let me know as a matter of urgency what your future intentions are in respect of this agreement.

Yours faithfully,

* *Is there an extortionate rate of interest?*

If you find you have been charged a very high rate of interest, it may make your agreement an 'extortionate credit bargain' under the Consumer Credit Act 1974. For further details see Chapter 2 (p. 42). It is possible to apply to the county court for the agreement to be reopened, and if the court agrees that the rate of interest is extortionate, the court can alter the terms of the agreement and in particular can reduce the amount of interest to be charged.

Before raising this issue take further advice.

* *Are the goods defective?*

Under the Sale of Goods Act 1979 you already have some rights against the supplier of defective goods. A supplier is not always the same person or company who grants you credit to purchase the goods. The Consumer Credit Act 1974 gives the borrower certain rights against the creditor in addition to the supplier where the goods are defective. It is essential that you take *immediate* action when you discover the defect. Write and tell the supplier AND creditor that the goods are defective and that you are taking legal advice.

Here is a suggested letter to write to the creditor in this situation:

Dear Sirs,

Re: Account No. 614/MPA/215

On 3 September 1986 I purchased a three-piece suite from the Shoddy Furniture Company at 182 High Street, Kitebridge, with credit provided by your company, on the above account number.

I now discover that the goods are defective and I am taking legal advice about my remedies against both the supplier and yourself. In the meantime I shall continue to make payments under the agreement.

Yours faithfully,

---

* *Were any misrepresentations made to you about the goods that you bought on credit?*

If a supplier makes representations about goods or services that turn out to be completely untrue, then the purchaser has rights under the Misrepresentation Act 1967. The Consumer Credit Act 1974 extends these rights so that, in certain circumstances, the creditor may be liable. Again, this is a situation where you need to take further qualified advice – from a legal aid solicitor, law centre, Citizens' Advice Bureau or consumer advice centre.

* *Can you apply for a time order under the Consumer Credit Act?*

If you are having difficulties making payments under your agreement, the Consumer Credit Act gives you

the right in certain circumstances to apply to the court
for further time to pay. This applies to both secured and
unsecured loans (see Chapter 9 for further details).
However, if your creditor has not yet taken you to
court, it is worth considering following the other procedures in this chapter *before* applying for a time order.

If having considered your legal position you are satisfied that none of these situations apply to you, then you
must prepare to negotiate with your creditors using:

* your Financial Statement including priority debts,

* a list of your debts

* a repayment programme.

Drafting a Repayment Programme

Your Financial Statement will show your final disposable income that is available to repay your non-
priority creditors.

You first need to add up all you individual debts to
give a figure for total indebtedness. You then divide
your disposable income between the creditors in proportion to the amount of each debt. Most creditors
work on a monthly basis, and so it is advisable to
calculate your offers on a monthly basis first of all.

This is the mathematical formula you should use
with each debt to calculate how much you can afford to
offer:

$$\frac{\text{Individual debt}}{\text{Total debt}} \times \frac{\text{Disposable}}{\text{income}} = \text{Monthly offer.}$$

Here is how Robert and Debbie Hunt calculated their
repayment programme:

Robert and Debbie have debts to five creditors as follows:

Johnsons Clothing Catalogue	168
Micawber Trust Finance	1,061
Flexible Bank Card	698
Merchandise Credit	260
Easicheck	153
Total	£2,340

They have £40 per month disposable income to divide between their creditors. The mathematical formula enables them to make an offer that is fair to each creditor.

The calculation works in this way with Johnsons and then each other creditor:

$$\text{Johnsons} \quad \frac{168}{2,340} \times 40 = £2.87$$

The Hunts rounded their repayment up or down to the nearest 50p and had a repayment programme that looked like this:

Creditor	Debt	Proportion of £40 per month
Johnsons	168	3.00
Micawber	1,061	18.00
Flexible	698	12.00
Merchandise	260	4.50
Easicheck	153	2.50
	£2,340	£40.00

The Hunts had now calculated how much they could afford to offer each creditor, but before putting the offer to their creditors they had to check whether the amount they were offering was more than the on-going interest. You need to do the same, particularly if you are being charged on-going interest on revolving credit accounts. We can look again at Robert and Debbie's situation:

The Hunts' debt to Flexible Bank Card Co. is a revolving credit account. Flexible have informed them that interest is accruing at £15.35 per month. Robert and Debbie can afford to offer only £12.00 per month, which means that the debt would increase at over £3 per month and not decrease at all. They cannot increase their offer to Flexible since this would be unfair to the other creditors, and they cannot afford more than £40 per month in total. There is only one solution, Robert and Debbie will have to ask Flexible to freeze or suspend further interest charges. If Flexible agree, the debt will be frozen at £698 and the £12 per month will reduce the total outstanding each month until the debt is cleared.

Creditors are prepared to consider this type of proposal on revolving credit accounts because they would often prefer to have a regular payment and give the borrower the incentive to pay by seeing the debt decrease every month. If the company refuse to accept the offer, they may have to sue to enforce the debt and incur the costs of court proceedings, only to find the court confirming the offer as reasonable in the circumstances.

When making proposals for reduced payment, you will need to return any credit card to the company concerned, cut into two halves so that the card cannot be stolen and used by somebody else.

It is unlikely that a finance company would agree to freeze further interest if the offer on the repayment programme substantially exceeded the monthly interest. However, in a borderline case – for example, where interest was accruing at £10 per month and the offer was £10.50 per month – creditors should be asked to agree to freezing further interest.

When you have calculated your repayment programme you can circulate your proposals to your creditors with your Financial Statement and a covering letter. If you wish to avoid creditors contacting each other about your case, you should refer in your repayment programme to the type of credit and not the actual company.

Remember!
You should have been honest with creditors when applying for the loan and made full disclosure of all existing agreements.

The Hunts programme would look like this:

Mr and Mrs Hunt		
Creditor	*Debt*	*Proportion of £40 per month*
Catalogue	168	3.00
Finance company	1,061	18.00
Bank card	698	12.00
Credit sale agreement	260	4.50
Check trading co.	153	2.50
	£2,340	£40.00

Two types of covering letter need to be sent, one for debts where no interest or service charges are being incurred, and the other for those such as revolving credit accounts where they are.

Robert and Debbie Hunt send the following letter to Johnsons Clothing Catalogue, Micawber Trust Finance Merchandise Credit and Easicheck:

64 South Street,
Kitebridge,
Pentshire.

Dear Sir,

Re: Account No. 6243/H23/84

I am enclosing a Financial Statement showing my present income and essential outgoings, including mortgage and rates arrears. The figure of £15 per week for miscellaneous expenditure covers repairs, replacements, health expenses, school expenses, entertainment, birthdays and Christmas. My income has reduced considerably since I commenced the above agreement due to loss of all overtime. I am left with a disposable income of £40 per month, which I intend to divide between my creditors in accordance with the enclosed repayment programme.

Please confirm that these arrangements are acceptable to you, so that payments can commence as soon as possible.

Yours faithfully,

To Flexible they send the following letter:

64 South Street,
Kitebridge,
Pentshire.

Dear Sir,

Re: Account No. 5240/6123/9240

I am enclosing a Financial Statement showing my present income and essential outgoings, including mortgage and rates arrears. The figure of £15 per week for miscellaneous expenditure covers repairs, replacements, health expenses, school expenses, entertainment, birthdays and Christmas. My income has reduced considerably since I commenced the above agreement due to loss of all overtime. I am left with a disposable income of £40 per month, which I intend to divide between my creditors in accordance with the enclosed repayment programme.

Unfortunately the £12 per month which I can afford to offer you does not cover the accruing interest, which you notified me is being added to my account at £15.35 per month at the moment. Since I cannot afford more than £12 per month without being unfair to my other creditors, please will you agree to freeze the account at £698.00 and suspend all further interest charges to enable me to clear this debt.

I am enclosing my Flexible Card cut in half with this letter. I look forward to hearing from you in the near future that this arrangement is acceptable to you so that payments can commence as soon as possible.

Yours faithfully,

Do not try to negotiate about your debts over the telephone except in emergencies. Large credit companies use sophisticated computer systems and will only reprogram their computers when they have exact details of your proposals in writing and they have accepted them.

If it is possible to visit your creditor's office you can negotiate a new arrangement face to face, but you will need to confirm the agreement in writing, so that each side knows exactly what the position is.

The Negotiations

If all your creditors accept your offers and agree to suspend further interest, all you have to do is start paying and keep it up until the debts are cleared. As replies come in however, it is more likely that some creditors will refuse to accept your proposals.

Creditors are bound to be suspicious of proposals that reduce the payments they are to receive. If a large number of their borrowers attempted to negotiate reduced payments or to freeze interest charges, the company would cease to make a profit and ultimately become insolvent. You may also have a bad payment record, which can only add to the creditor's scepticism. It may take some time and effort to persuade the credit-granter that you are genuine and not trying to 'pull a fast one'. If you feel nervous and at a disadvantage asking for help in this way, try to remember that this is a situation that is equally unwelcome to creditors.

When you have replies from your creditors, there are six possible positions.

All creditors accept

Start paying immediately at the agreed rate. If your circumstances change again for the better, increase your payments to get the debt repaid sooner. If your circumstances change for the worse and you cannot continue to pay at the agreed rate, inform your creditors *immediately*. When creditors accept they often set a time limit, for example 12 months, and state that they will review the position then. You will need to provide an up-to-date Financial Statement setting out your current income and outgoings so that they can consider whether to continue the arrangement.

All creditors refuse

You need to ask why. Was your Financial Statement correct? Go back and check your outgoings to see if there are any further economies that you can reasonably be expected to make. If you have made your best offer, and all creditors have refused to accept, you may have to resign yourself to court proceedings being commenced against you. You can then make your offer to the court, which will have to decide whether it is fair.

Some creditors refuse

If a creditor refuses your offer without explanation, you should write again and ask for the reasons for refusal. This will sometimes prompt the creditor to look again, perhaps more carefully, at your offer, and may result in an acceptance. The most common reason for refusing an offer is that expenditure on non-essential items such as cigarettes, car, video, telephone and entertainment can be reduced to increase the offer to creditors. You must therefore be able to justify expenditure on these items. If you feel that the creditor is being unfair, write again, setting out your position.

Whilst carrying on negotiations with those who have refused, start paying those who have accepted immediately. Do not miss a payment.

A majority accept

If you have calculated your offers fairly, we hope that the majority of your creditors will accept your proposals, which will put you in a strong bargaining position with the minority who have refused. You need to tell a creditor who refuses that he is in a minority and ask him to reconsider. If he sees that other creditors are accepting, this can help to persuade him that he is being unreasonable in refusing.

Do not offer a difficult creditor more money. If you do, it throws doubt on the honesty of your first offer. The creditor will think you have lied and have some spare income that you can use to pay, or that you can spend less than you first said was essential. It is also unfair to those creditors who have accepted.

A creditor refuses to suspend interest

It is possible that a creditor with whom you have a revolving credit account, or where interest charges continue to accrue, will accept your repayment offer but refuse to suspend further interest charges. If interest is being added at a greater rate than you are able to pay the debt off, this is not going to help you get clear. This is one of the most difficult situations to have to deal with since the creditor is perfectly entitled legally to carry on charging interest. The creditor will need to be persuaded that it is in his interests to suspend interest, at least temporarily, to provide the borrower with some incentive to pay.

THE HUNTS

Johnsons and Easicheck accept without too much difficulty. They are fixed-term agreements with interest built in at the beginning and they will recover capital plus interest, but over a longer period of time than normal. Micawber Finance were initially reluctant to accept but, since they were getting more than anyone else, decided to accept for 12 months and then review the position, in the hope that Robert Hunt might get a pay rise or more opportunities for overtime in a year's time. Merchandise Credit refused to accept £4.50 per month, and Flexible stated they would not accept £12 and could not suspend the interest charges, which were accruing at over £15 per month. Robert and Debbie composed the following letters:

To Merchandise Credit Co. Ltd

64 South Street,
Kitebridge,
Pentshire.

Dear Sirs,

Re: Account No. 246 CS 84 1009

Thank you for your letter of 10 October 1986, concerning the above account.

I am sorry that you feel unable to accept the offer which I have made. The majority of the other creditors have accepted the offers made to them and I have commenced payments. I cannot offer you more because I can only afford £40 per month between all my creditors, and it would be wrong to cease or reduce payments to accepting creditors in favour of your company.

In the light of other creditors agreeing to the

repayment plan, please would you reconsider my offer.

   Yours faithfully,

To Flexible Bank Card PLC

                              64 South Street,
                              Kitebridge,
                              Pentshire.

Dear Sirs,

Re: Account No. 5240/6123/9240

   Thank you for your letter of 12 October 1986 concerning the above account.

   I am sorry that you feel unable to suspend interest charges on the above account. The majority of my creditors have agreed to the repayment programme and I have commenced payments to them. I cannot pay you £25 per month as requested since I only have £40 per month available to divide between all my creditors, and it would be wrong to cease or reduce payments to creditors who have already accepted my offer.

   You have already charged considerable sums of interest to the above account, and even with all future interest suspended it will take my wife and me nearly five years to pay off what we owe to all our creditors, unless my circumstances change for the better. We believe that our Financial Statement shows that we cannot afford more at the present time, and we would ask you to reconsider your decision in the light of the fact that other creditors have agreed to accept our offer.

   Yours faithfully,

A creditor refuses to accept despite all your efforts

A few creditors will refuse to accept your offer in spite of all your efforts. There will come a point when you will have to give up trying to negotiate and invite the creditor to use his legal sanction and sue you in the courts. The main disadvantage of being sued is that you will have a court order against you, plus the court costs to pay. The main advantage is that the court is likely to accept offers to repay made in good faith and calculated on a pro rata basis, having regard to your essential outgoings. What is more, if interest is accruing on your account, it will cease when a judgment is made against you for the debt, unless you are sued in the High Court. Inviting a creditor to take you to court can persuade him to cooperate with your offer, since it shows that you understand the legal position and your legal rights in the matter.

This is the letter Robert Hunt would have to write to Flexible if they continue to refuse his offer:

---

64 South Street,
Kitebridge,
Pentshire.

Dear Sir,

Re: Account No. 5240/6123/9240

Thank you for your letter of 31 October 1986. I am very disappointed that we seem unable to reach a satisfactory compromise in this case. As I have already explained, I can only afford £12 per month at the present time, and I feel that it is pointless paying this amount to you only to see my debt increase. I invite you therefore to sue me for the debt, when I shall have the opportunity of offering £12 per month through the courts.

In addition, once judgment is granted I understand that further interest will be suspended in any event. It seems that we can only achieve a reasonable outcome to this matter by allowing the courts to decide, although this will involve us

> both in extra expense and time wasted at court hearings.
>
> My offer of £12 per month plus suspension of interest is of course still open to you to accept.
>
> Yours faithfully,

If the creditor still refuses to accept, you should consider applying for a time order yourself under the Consumer Credit Act. Tell the creditor you are thinking of taking this course, as it may persuade him to think again, but do not suggest it unless you are prepared to follow it through by commencing proceedings (which will cost approximately £30) to ask the court to reduce the instalments to what you can afford.

If you feel that a time order is inappropriate in your case, then you will have to consider forcing your creditor to take you to court by simply not paying him at all. Court proceedings are considered fully in Chapter 9.

Remember!

If the creditor does sue you and obtains a judgment against you, your name will appear on a credit blacklist.

Persuading Creditors to Cooperate

There are some steps that you can take to try to achieve maximum cooperation from your creditors.

* The most important is to keep writing to them. Do not be put off by the first refusal. Keep them fully informed and find as many reasons as possible for writing to them so that they know you are still trying to reach a compromise.

* If the first letter is signed by a clerk or assistant, write again, but this time address the letter to the Arrears Manager. Normally, the higher up you go the more

authority there is to make an exception to the general
rule.

---

* Keep your letters short and to the point, but do not be
afraid to explain *why* you have got into debt. Creditors
tend to be more sympathetic if there is a good reason
such as unemployment, sickness, marital breakdown,
or an unexpected expense.

---

* Many people feel nervous about negotiating with
creditors. If that is so, it may be helpful to ask someone
to assist you in your negotiations. In addition, creditors
often feel more confident if they have some independent person confirming that the information on income
and outgoings is true and accurate. The best people to
approach are money advisers or debt workers who are
found in money advice centres, and in some Citizens'
Advice Bureaux, law centres and consumer advice
centres. Unfortunately there are too few of them and
many areas of the country have none.

But there are other people who may be able to give
you some assistance, particularly in the area of assuring
creditors that you are telling them the truth. Most
Citizens' Advice Bureaux will have a volunteer who
can help you to write a letter. Other people who may
help you are:

- A legal aid solicitor
- your local city or county councillor
- your local MP
- social worker
- local community worker
- probation officer
- local authority housing officer or advice worker
- staff welfare officer at work
- vicar or priest
- your employer (unless it is inadvisable to tell him
  of your debts)
- a friend or relative in a professional post.

These people may be prepared to help you prepare your Financial Statement and your offer to creditors if you cannot do it yourself. With an uncooperative creditor, a letter from an independent person confirming that your figures are true can make all the difference in persuading them to accept the realities of your situation and your offer.

☞ **Warning!**
Be careful of anyone who offers to negotiate with your creditors for a fee. They may be operating at the fringes of the law, and may become just another creditor if you find you cannot afford their fees.

Some Points on Payment

Once agreement has been reached, payments must be made promptly and regularly on the agreed date. A late or inaccurate payment can cause the trust between you and a creditor to break down.

It is important to consider *how* you are going to pay:

* If your creditor employs a door-to-door collector, it is cheap and convenient to pay cash.

* If you budget weekly, it may suit you to pay one-quarter of your monthly figure each week by calling at your creditor's local office.

* If you have to pay by postal order, cheque or standing order on your bank account, it is cheaper to pay monthly. The banker's order and cheque should be paid on a date when you know there will be enough money in your account to cover it.

* You can spread payments throughout the month by paying one creditor in the first week and the others in subsequent weeks. For example:

Debbie and Robert Hunt have monthly payments to make to five creditors. They spread them like this:

FEBRUARY

Week 1
Micawber Trust   £18.00

Week 2
Johnsons Catalogue   £3.00
Easicheck   £2.50

Week 3
Flexible   £12.00

Week 4
Merchandise Credit   £4.50

---

* If you do not have a bank account, the Post Office Transcash system can be a cheaper way of paying than by postal order. Find out more from your local Post Office. Some building societies will pay standing orders on your account without making any charge at all.

Long-term consequences of Reducing Payments

* You will not be able to have any further credit from these creditors. Most credit card companies will ask for the return of the card. In addition, these creditors are unlikely to want to do business with you again in the future even when you have paid off your debt to them.

* You may find yourself on a credit blacklist as a credit defaulter. This will make it much more difficult for you to get low-cost credit in the future, at least until the debts are cleared. You will have to resign yourself to the fact that credit is not for you for some considerable

time, unless you pay a great deal for it – which is hardly
advisable.

* You may find these restrictions hard to accept after a
time, particularly once the initial relief of solving your
present problem has worn off. You may be tempted to
improve your standard of living by using credit again.
New credit commitments MUST NOT be entered into
until you have paid what you owe.

What to Do if There Is No Disposable Income for Unsecured Creditors

For borrowers on a low wage or in receipt of state
benefits, or for those with very large priority debts,
there may be no disposable income left at the end of the
Financial Statement for unsecured creditors.

If this is your case you have to write to your creditors
and explain the situation. Ask them to freeze interest
and service charges until you can pay again, either
when you return to work or when you have paid off
your priority debts.

Here is a suggested letter.

---

64 South Street,
Kitebridge,
Pentshire.

Dear Sir,

Re: Account No. 5220/6143/9127

On 6 September 1986 I was made redundant.
Unfortunately I had only been with the company
for eighteen months and I did not qualify for a
redundancy payment. My family and I are now
living on a much reduced income, as you can see
from the Financial Statement which I enclose.
After payment of the mortgage, food, fuel and
other essential items I do not have any income
remaining to pay on the above account.

> In the circumstances, please will you consider suspending further interest charges and accepting nil repayments until I have found another job. I am a skilled plumber and hope to be able to find employment in the near future. I shall keep you informed of my efforts to find work, and will recommence payments as soon as my income improves. In the meantime I hope that you can accede to my requests so that I will have a fixed sum to repay rather than an escalating debt.
>
> I am also writing to my other creditors asking them to accept the same arrangement.
>
> I look forward to hearing from you in the near future.
>
> Yours faithfully,

In these circumstances it is extremely important to write regularly and keep the creditor informed of job opportunities, interviews, etc. If you have not managed to obtain work within a reasonable period of time, you might need to ask the creditor to consider 'writing off' all or part of the debt.

Getting Debts 'Written off'

Understandably creditors are reluctant to write off bad debts. However, there are circumstances where they may feel it is pointless pursuing a debt.

LONG-TERM UNEMPLOYED

Where a borrower becomes unemployed and is never likely to work again – perhaps because of age, disability and/or the high levels of unemployment in the area – that borrower will probably have to rely on state benefits until retirement age. In these circumstances it is often not worthwhile for a creditor to continue to pursue a debt when there is little or no prospect of receiving a substantial payment.

SINGLE PARENTS

Where a borrower is unable to work due to having to care for a child or children, and that situation is likely to continue for a number of years.

DEATH OR SEPARATION

Where there is a joint agreement and the earning partner dies or leaves and cannot be traced, the creditor may decide not to pursue the debt against the remaining joint-borrower, if that person has no income save state benefits, and no earning capacity for reasons such as age, sickness or disability.

WRITING OFF PART OF A DEBT

Where a repayment programme is calculated and it will take the borrower many years to pay off the debts, it is sometimes possible to persuade creditors to accept payment over a reduced number of years, in effect writing off part of the debt. For example:

> Robert and Debbie Hunt have debts of £2,340. If Robert is aged 55 and Debbie can no longer work due to ill-health and there is no prospect of Robert achieving further promotion, and the most they can afford to all creditors is £12 per month, it will take them over 16 years to repay their debts. Apart from the fact that Robert will retire in 10 years' time, most creditors would agree that a repayment programme over 16 years provides very little incentive for Robert and Debbie to pay. To provide an incentive and to give them a future hope of freedom from indebtedness, creditors may be persuaded to accept payments for a five-year period only, making total repayments of £720 and writing off the outstanding balance of £1,620.

BANKRUPTCY

See Chapter 9.

Debts to Relatives

As we discussed in Chapters 4 and 5, borrowing from
relatives can have unfortunate consequences, especially
if there is no clear agreement covering the terms on
which the loan is made.

Some readers may already have borrowed money
from friends and relatives to try and solve their debt
problems. It is often felt that these debts carry a moral
obligation to repay over and above debts to other
creditors, either priority or unsecured. This must remain an area for individual decision. However, most
commercial creditors will be unwilling to accept
reduced payments if they see another unsecured
creditor, albeit a relative, receiving preferential treatment. As a general principle, a debt to a friend or
relative should be treated in exactly the same way as
other unsecured debts and included in a repayment
programme. Such a debt should not receive preferential repayment unless there are exceptional circumstances that would justify preference being given. On
the other hand, just because the loan was made verbally
does not mean that it should be ignored. It is equally
enforceable at law whether it was made verbally or in
writing.

Conclusion

Even though unsecured debts do not have the drastic
consequences that priority debts attract, borrowers still
have a responsibility to make repayments where possible, to attempt to negotiate an agreement, and then
keep to it. Equally, creditors have a responsibility to
look realistically at the situations in which borrowers
find themselves. If credit is advanced on the basis of
future income being used to repay, and if that income
falls short of what is expected, this requires adjustments from both sides to the agreement. The repayment programmes suggested in this chapter can only
work if the borrower is truthful with the creditor, and if
the creditor is reasonable and realistic in his dealings
with the borrower.

9

Using the Courts and Bankruptcy

We hope that by using Chapters 4–8 of this book you will have negotiated agreements with your creditors and avoided the necessity of going to court altogether. However, if court proceedings are started against you, you are not alone – nearly 2 million actions are commenced every year in England and Wales alone for debt or debt-related matters.

Court proceedings are normally started by creditors but it is important to remember that creditors are often reluctant to involve the courts. Most unsecured creditors will consider court proceedings as a last resort, to be turned to when they cannot reach an agreement with, or get a reply from, debtors. Others threaten court proceedings to try and persuade you to pay more, without having any real intention of going to court.

The disadvantages of going to court for creditors are:

* the cost of proceedings;

* the length of time it takes, sometimes weeks or months, before anything gets decided;

* the fact that, if properly informed, the court will take the borrower's side into account, and the creditor may

end up with smaller instalments than he could get by simply threatening a frightened debtor with 'court'.

Your Feelings about Courts

The most common feelings people have about courts and court proceedings are worry and fear. There can be no doubt that courts may be frightening and intimidating places, particularly if you do not understand what is going on. Court forms and letters are often unintelligible to the person in the street, and this adds to the temptation not to answer or fill in the forms for fear of writing or doing the wrong thing.

Many people on the receiving end of court proceedings do not know where best to go to get advice and end up doing nothing. Others assume that once the courts are involved the outcome will be unfavourable to them, whatever they do, so give up trying to resolve their problems. Many debtors worry about the expense of going to court or taking advice and do not wish to add to their financial problems by incurring what they often assume is further expense.

Most of these fears are either ill-founded or can be resolved once you understand how the courts work. It is thus important to remember the following basic points:

* Many creditors do not *want* to use court action if it can be avoided.

* Even when court proceedings have been started, you can still attempt to negotiate with your creditor.

* If you respond to court proceedings by filling in forms or attending hearings when asked to, you are likely to achieve a *better* result for yourself than if you do nothing.

* Do not be frightened of the courts, they can sometimes be *your* friend. They are not there to serve the interests

of creditors, they are there to ensure that justice is done between lender and borrower.

* The courts can be particularly helpful to a debtor where the creditor has been difficult or unreasonable.

* Although court costs do get added on to the debt, the quicker you respond the less the costs are likely to be. Creditors cannot charge what costs they like; these are assessed on a sliding scale set by the courts, according to the amount of the debt.

* Creditors are often unable to charge all their court expenses to the debtor, which is a good reason for asking them not to commence proceedings in the first place.

* Legal aid is available for some proceedings, but, more importantly, you can get *advice* from a solicitor under the legal aid scheme. This will either cost you nothing, £5 (ask for a fixed-fee interview) or a small amount under the Green Form scheme. If you decide to approach a solicitor, always ask him how much he is going to charge *before* you start the interview.

* Money advice centres, law centres, consumer advice centres, and Citizens' Advice Bureaux can all give you *free* advice about court forms and court proceedings.

General Principles in Court

THE PURPOSE OF THE COURTS

The courts' objective is to provide independent arbitration between two opposing parties. The court has to decide whether the money is owed, and if so, how it should be paid. If security has been given for a loan (e.g. a mortgage), the court has to decide whether to allow the creditor to enforce the debt by taking the security.

THE PERSONNEL IN THE COURTS
Broadly speaking, there are two categories:

- the civil servants who do all the administrative work, prepare the papers for court, usher people around the building, and staff the court office,

- the judicial staff – the Judges, Registrars, and Sheriffs in Scotland – who actually make the decisions concerning the disputes between the parties.

What the courts can do
The court can rarely initiate proceedings itself. It normally has to wait until one party or the other brings a particular matter of dispute before it to decide. Since creditors start most proceedings, it can look as if the court is there just to serve the creditors' interests. However, if debtors come to court to tell the adjudicator their side of the case, it obviously helps the court to reach a fairer decision. In cases where the debtor does not present his side of the argument because he does not fill in the court forms or attend the hearing, it is difficult for the court to reach a balanced decision. In these circumstances the court usually has no option but to do what the creditor asks.

The System in England and Wales

In England and Wales, debts other than fines, rates and some maintenance arrears are dealt with in the county court and High Court. These are purely *civil* courts, where no criminal business is transacted, and the adjudicators are called Registrars and Judges. Most debt cases are dealt with by Registrars either in open court (a public hearing) or in chambers (informally in the Registrar's private office). There will be no publicity as the media are not interested in cases such as these.

Where the debt is less than £5,000 (£15,000 in the case of regulated agreements under the Consumer Credit Act 1974), proceedings should be started in the county court. If proceedings are commenced in the High Court a defendant should see a solicitor *immediately*. After a High Court writ has been served, a defendant has only *14 days* in which to take action. Fortunately most debt cases take place in the county court, where proceedings are more suited to the ordinary person who is conducting his case without legal representation.

Proceedings in the county court are started by the credit-granter (the plaintiff) sending to the borrower (the defendant) a summons which is normally accompanied by a document called 'particulars of claim', which sets out the plaintiff's case in some detail. Also sent to the defendant is a document to fill in and return to the court. Costs are added on to the debt at the time of issuing the summons. It is difficult to avoid paying these costs unless you can show that the plaintiff was wholly unreasonable in commencing the proceedings.

Possession proceedings:
rent arrears/mortgage arrears/secured loan arrears
When default has occurred in rent, mortgage or secured loan payments, the creditor (plaintiff) commences possession proceedings by issuing a **possession summons**.

Before issuing the summons the creditor who is suing for:

---

* *rent arrears* must have issued a notice of intention to seek possession or a notice to quit the premises, so you will already be warned court action is in view;

---

* *secured loan arrears* must issue a default notice under the Consumer Credit Act;

---

* *mortgage arrears* normally issues a notice calling in the whole loan including the arrears.

ACTION TO TAKE
☞ When you receive a possession summons it will have on it a **hearing date**. It is most important that you note the date and make arrangements to attend.

☞ It will also have with it a **form N.11**. The main question
on the form is whether you admit that the plaintiff is
entitled to take possession of the premises. It is best to
answer 'No'. Then there is a space for setting out your
side of the case. Here you should explain:

- why you got into arrears
- your proposals for paying back the money you
  owe
- your family circumstances.

The second part of the form asks whether you admit
any claim for money by the plaintiff. Work out whether
you agree that you owe what the plaintiff says you owe.
If you do not agree, say so on this part of the form, and
say *why* you dispute the claim.

☞ Send the Form N.11 back to the court with a copy of
your Financial Statement *within 14 days* of receiving the
summons.

Remember!
You can still negotiate with the plaintiff, and if you can
reach an agreement the hearing date can be adjourned
generally by consent of both plaintiff and defendant to
give the agreement a chance to work.

If you cannot make an agreement you will have to
attend at court on the hearing date. Take to the hearing
a copy of your Financial Statement and a schedule of
your other debts.

Where your home is at risk, it may be possible for
you to get *legal aid* to be represented by a solicitor at
court; if not, you may be able to get an advice worker to
attend court with you.

Your case is likely to be in a long list of other similar
cases. The Registrar will only spend about five minutes
on your case and although the hearing is usually in
open court there will be no publicity in the newspapers. The plaintiff will usually be represented by a
solicitor or barrister. Find out from the court usher
which is the plaintiff's representative and introduce

yourself. Make sure you tell the usher that you are at the court and in which case you are involved. You should call the Registrar 'Sir' or 'Madam'.

At the hearing the Registrar can make one of the following orders:

- An order dismissing the plaintiff's action, e.g. where all the arrears have been cleared before the hearing date, OR the plaintiff has failed to establish his case.

- An order adjourning (putting off) the case generally (for an unspecified length of time) or for a specified length of time, e.g. three months or to another fixed date.

- An order that the case be adjourned subject to conditions of repayment by the borrower.

- An order that possession of the property be given to the plaintiff, but suspended or postponed on conditions that the court feels appropriate, normally on condition that the rent or mortgage is paid regularly, *plus* a payment off the arrears.

- An order for outright possession of the property to take effect within a specified length of time, normally 28 days.

If you admit the arrears you should make an offer of repayment that you can afford, calculated under the system set out in Chapters 5–7. In that case the Registrar is likely to make a suspended order of possession.

If you can repay the whole of the arrears within a relatively short space of time, e.g. three months, you should try for an adjournment.

In the case of mortgage arrears and secured loan arrears, if you cannot make any payment at all (because, for example, you are on benefit) ask for an adjournment to try and sell the house yourself, rather than letting the plaintiff take possession, evict you, and sell it.

In the case of rent arrears, if you cannot afford a substantial payment offer £1 per week off the arrears.

Courts are likely to grant tenants a longer period of time over which to pay off rent arrears than mortgage arrears.

Remember!
Once an agreement has been made you must keep to it. If you cannot, you must go back to the court and ask for the order to be varied.

If you do not or cannot pay under the order, the plaintiff will have the case re-listed for hearing, and ask the court for a **warrant of possession**. If the court grants the warrant, an eviction date will be fixed. Even at this stage you can apply for the warrant to be suspended if you can make a substantial offer to pay off the arrears, or can show that you have a buyer for the property. If you do not leave the property, the bailiffs will attend on the appointed day and physically evict you and your family from the premises. They are not obliged to remove the furniture and so to recover your possessions you will have to get the plaintiff's agreement to re-enter the property in the future to arrange for removal of your furniture.

In the case of mortgage arrears, after the eviction the plaintiff will sell the property, pay off all the costs, expenses, estate agents' and solicitors' fees, the mortgage and any second or third mortgages, and will return any surplus money to you. You are entitled to an account of the disposal of the money.

Where the plaintiff is a building society, a statutory obligation is imposed to obtain the best available price for the property at the time the building society chooses to sell. Banks and finance companies are not under a similar statutory duty, but must act in 'good faith' in the sale, which means that they must act honestly. Obviously a forced sale by a lender is likely to produce a lower selling price than if the owner sells.

Hire purchase proceedings
The owner of the goods will issue a **fixed-date summons**, asking for repossession of the goods. This is only

necessary where *more* than one-third of the hire purchase price has been paid, and after the owner has
served the notices required under the Consumer Credit
Act. You will also receive a **Form N.10** to fill in stating
whether you dispute the claim or not.

☞ It is advisable at this stage to seek legal advice because
you might have a defence.

If you do not have a defence, fill in Page 1 of Form N.10,
which is basically a means enquiry. The most important part of the form is at the bottom – where you are
asked whether the goods are still in your possession
(they should be) and what offer of payment you make.
Calculate your offer as set out in Chapter 8 because this
debt now ranks with the other unsecured debts. Send
the form back to the court within 14 days with a
Financial Statement and a schedule of your other debts,
so that the court can see how you have calculated your
offer.

The court will forward a copy of the Form N.10 to the
plaintiff. If he agrees to accept your offer it may not be
necessary for you to attend at the hearing. If this is the
case you will be notified.

If you hear nothing, this means that the case is
proceeding to a hearing. Attend the hearing where the
court will decide whether repossession should take
place, or whether you should retain the goods and
make a reduced instalment payment. The court is more
likely to make an order for repossession if the goods are
a car, other vehicle or very expensive electrical goods
than if the goods are furniture, carpets or smaller electrical items that have virtually no second-hand value.

If repossession is ordered, or you should subse-
quently fail to make the agreed payments, then the
court can issue a **warrant of recovery** entitling the
plaintiff to repossess the goods. Even at this stage you
can apply to the court for the warrant to be suspended
by making an offer to pay.

Unsecured debts

The creditor without security for his debt must use a completely different procedure. Here the task is not to try to recover possession of goods or of a house but to enforce the debt by getting the court to make the borrower pay.

This time proceedings are started by the creditor (the plaintiff) issuing a **default summons** through the county court. The creditor can do this only *after* the service of a **default notice** to the debtor under the Consumer Credit Act.

The default summons comes to you with a **Form N.9** and often also with a 'particulars of claim' setting out the plaintiff's case. This summons does *not* fix a date for the hearing. The purpose is to give you the chance to put your side of the case. It is *vital* that you complete Form N.9 and send it back to the court. If Form N.9 is not sent back the case goes by default.

The Form N.9 has two sides. Side 2 is for defendants who wish to dispute the plaintiff's claim, in which case you are best advised to take legal advice. Side 1 of the form deals with defendants who agree that they owe the money but want further time in which to pay it back. You can get legal aid for advice on how to fill the form in, but you cannot get legal aid to be represented in court if you admit that you owe the money and the only issue is how it shall be paid. Side 1 of the Form N.9 is also a means enquiry. It is the court's way of finding out what your income, outgoings and other debts are.

The bottom of Form N.9 is the *most important* part, entitled 'What offer of payment do you make?' Offer *only* what you can realistically afford. Creditors have been known to accept as little as 50p per month where it could be established that no more money could be reasonably afforded. If you are living on state benefits, 50p is the sort of offer you should consider making, especially where you have priority debts.

If you do not know how much you *can* afford because – for example, you are waiting for other creditors to let you know how much you owe them before you can apportion your disposable income between all your creditors – make a nominal offer of £1 per month and explain the position in a covering letter, telling the court that you hope to be in a position to make a better offer in the near future when you have all the relevant information.

Return the form within 14 days if possible and send with it a copy of your Financial Statement, including priority debts, and a schedule of your other debts, showing the amounts you owe and the proportion of your disposable income that you intend to allocate to each debt.

The court will then send all the information to the creditor, who will look at your offer and if it is considered reasonable will probably accept it. The court will notify you of the acceptance and in these circumstances you will not have to go to court. What you will have to do is to commence making payments on the date given to you by the court, and to make your payments into the court Office regularly every month.

If the plaintiff does not accept your offer, the court will fix a **hearing date** for the court to decide how much the instalments should be, or whether you should be ordered to pay the whole amount immediately. You will then be notified of the hearing date. If it is inconvenient you can try and get it adjourned. However, it is *very important* that you attend. The hearing will be in public but there will be no publicity.

Take along your Financial Statement, schedule of other debts, and if possible some proof of your earnings – a pay slip or salary advice. If possible introduce yourself to the plaintiff's representative, but do not allow him to push you into offering more than you can afford; stick to the offer that you made on the Form N.9. Tell the usher or court clerk that you are at court, so that they can tell the Registrar that you are present.

At the hearing the Registrar has to decide whether your offer is reasonable. Do not be frightened to justify the offer that you have made to the Registrar. They may ask you questions about your income and about opportunities for overtime. They may want to know more about the outgoings that you have shown on your Financial Statement. Be ready to explain that a TV is a necessity – because, for example, you have children and it is a very cheap form of entertainment. The Registrar may also want further details of your other debts. Do tell the court if other creditors have accepted your proposals, as that will help the Registrar to decide the matter in your favour.

When the Registrar has made his decision, he will announce it there and then. You can then leave. Later, you will receive notification by post from the court.

The Registrar will have given what is called 'judgment' for the full amount owed, plus costs. He will make an order for payment, usually by monthly instalments, and after judgment no further interest will accrue on the debt. It is proposed to allow simple interest to be charged on county court judgments but a date for implementation has not been fixed.

If you fail to fill in the Form N.9, the creditor will apply for payment at the rate that he requires, which may be much more than you can afford. If you cannot pay, all is still not lost. At any time the court can be asked to vary the instalments that have been ordered.

To make an application for instalments to be reduced, get a **Form N.245** from your local county court office, fill it in, setting out why you need a reduction, e.g. a loss of overtime, and file it at the court Office with your Financial Statement and a schedule of your other debts.

OTHER ENFORCEMENT TECHNIQUES
If you fail to pay the whole amount within the specified time, or the instalments ordered, the plaintiff can look for other methods of enforcing the debt against you.

Oral examination

The plaintiff applies to the court to have you called before the court to give evidence concerning your income and assets. You must attend, otherwise you can be arrested and brought to court. The object of the procedure is to find out how much you are worth. It is an opportunity for you to make an offer of payment if you have not already started to pay.

Warrant of execution

If you miss payments, the plaintiff can apply for a warrant of execution, which authorises the county court bailiffs to come to your house and seize goods belonging to you to the value of the missed payments or of the judgment debt, plus the bailiffs' costs. The only goods exempted from seizure are beds, bedding, clothes and the tools of the trade, if any, up to a value of £250.

The bailiffs *should not*:

● break into your home,

● seize goods that do not belong to the *actual* defendant. They *should*:

● give you a list of everything that they are taking.

Bailiffs usually take what is called 'walking possession' of the goods they seize. This means that they leave them in your home for a period of time, normally seven days after the first visit, to give you an opportunity of making arrangements to pay. If you do not however, they will return in seven days, remove the goods on the list, and take them to an auction room where they will be sold. You or a relative or friend are free to bid for the goods at the sale.

You can normally avoid your goods being seized by:

* making a payment to the bailiffs who will pass it to the court Office,

* making an offer of regular payment,

* making *immediate* application on a Form N.245 for a suspension of the warrant. You will need to make an offer of repayment on the form.

If you apply for a suspension of the warrant and make a new offer to pay, the court will send the offer to the plaintiff, who can accept or reject it. If he rejects the offer, the court will fix a **hearing** for the Registrar to decide whether to let the sale go ahead or whether to suspend the warrant as a result of your offer to pay by instalments.

It is clearly unwise to let debt enforcement reach this stage. Normally you have no knowledge of a bailiff's visit before it takes place, and it can be a most unpleasant experience to open your door and find a bailiff preparing to examine everything that you own with a view to selling it.

If the bailiff finds that what you own will not cover the costs of a full execution and sale (approximately £100–150), the warrant will be returned to the court marked 'no goods', and that is the end of the procedure.

Attachment of earnings

The plaintiff applies through the court to have the instalments that you have been ordered to pay deducted from your pay before you receive it. Your employer is ordered by the court to pay a weekly or monthly deduction into court for the plaintiff's benefit, until the money owed is fully paid or you move jobs.

You will be asked to fill in a **Form N.56**, which asks for details of your employment, income, outgoings and debts. It is a good idea to send a Financial Statement and schedule of debts as well. At the bottom of the form you are asked: 'What sum would you be prepared to have deducted from your earnings to satisfy the plaintiff's judgment?' Here you should offer the figure that you have apportioned in your repayment programme to this creditor.

If you fill in the form, you do not have to attend the hearing, but it is still a good idea to attend because you may not want an attachment made. Many people feel that an attachment of earnings order alerts their employer to the fact that they have a court order against them, and this may prejudice their position at work. Other debtors, however, find it a most useful way of budgeting for paying off debts if the money is deducted from wages *before* they are paid over – any worry about payment is removed.

If the court insists on making an order, you can ask for it to be suspended to give you the opportunity to pay the instalments voluntarily. If you then fail to make payments the suspension will be lifted and the order will be sent to your employers.

At the hearing, the Registrar must set a 'protected earnings level', which should cover the basic essential outgoings on your Financial Statement. Deductions must never take your net pay below this protected earnings level. If your earnings ever fall below the protected level, no deduction can be made.

Charging order

This is an application made by a plaintiff with an unsatisfied judgment against a defendant who possesses a substantial capital asset, such as a house. If a charging order is made it will secure the judgment debt against the house/asset of the defendant, thus turning an unsecured loan into a secured debt. A plaintiff can apply for a charging order even where a defendant is paying his instalments regularly and at the amount ordered.

The Charging Orders Act 1979 provides that, *before* an order can be made, the court should consider all the circumstances of the case, and particularly:

- the personal circumstances of the debtor,

- whether another creditor might be prejudiced by the making of an order.

In practice we have found that, where the debtor is making a real effort to pay, or is in a dire financial position, or where there are multiple unsecured debts, the courts rarely make a charging order.

Once a charging order has been made, the plaintiff can then ask the court to order a sale of the property so that the debt can be paid off. In practice most courts try to avoid granting an order for sale when the defendant is living in the property, particularly if s/he has a family and is making some effort to pay by instalments.

Garnishee proceedings

A plaintiff with an unsatisfied judgment can apply

through the county court for a garnishee order. This orders a third party who owes money to or holds money on behalf of the defendant to pay it into court, and *not* to the defendant. The money can then go to pay the judgment debt. These actions are fairly rare.

Administration orders
We have seen that most county court proceedings are started by creditors. However, the county court also provides a method for payment of debts for which a defendant with a court judgment against him can apply. This is called a county court administration order. If granted, the order enables the debtor to consolidate his debts within the court system. You will be ordered to pay one monthly instalment into the county court Office. This will then be distributed pro rata to your creditors by the court after deduction of administrative costs (currently 10 per cent, i.e. 10p for each £1 of debt).

You can apply for an administration order if:

● your *total* debts are less than £5,000, *and*

● you have one or more county court judgments against you, *or*

● you have a High Court judgment against you and your *total* debts, including that judgment, are less than £5,000.

You apply for an administration order by filing **Form N.92** at Court. You have to give details of one judgment debt at the top of the form and then details of all your other debts on pages 1 and 2. On page 1 you also have to state how much per month you are proposing to offer to all your creditors. Page 3 of the form is a means enquiry, asking questions about income and outgoings. Fill it in and also enclose a copy of your Financial Statement.

When filling in the form bear these points in mind:

* A husband and wife cannot make a joint application. Each must first qualify to apply for an administration

order and then make an individual application on a separate form. For example:

David and Jane Keen have the following debts:

Catalogue	200	(Jane's debt)
Bank card	650	(David's debt)
Finance company	1,950	(Joint debt)
In-store credit card	320	(David's debt)
TOTAL	£3,120	

Thus Jane's debts are:

Catalogue	200
Finance company	1,950
TOTAL	£2,150

and David's debts are:

Bank card	650
Finance company	1,950
In-store credit card	320
TOTAL	£2,920

If the finance company obtain a judgment against both Jane and David, they can *both* apply for administration orders. If only the catalogue company obtains a judgment, only Jane can apply. If only the bank card company obtains a judgment, then only David can apply.

---

* Calculation of the £5,000 can cause difficulties. If you have a mortgage it is normal to exclude that from the

calculation. However, some county courts will insist
that it is included, which effectively prevents most
owner-occupiers from having an administration order.
In some courts it is the practice to exclude some priority
debts from the calculation, such as rates, fines and
maintenance arrears, since they are administered in a
different court.

You can check on the practice in your local court by
contacting the office of the Chief Clerk of the county
court.

* When you have filed your application for an administration order, all other enforcement proceedings (with
the possible exception of garnishee or charging order
proceedings) should be halted until the court has
considered the application. In other words, whilst
the application is pending it acts like an insurance
against creditors' enforcement and in particular
bailiffs' visits.

* Most courts will allow creditors to object to their particular debt being scheduled to an administration order and
will allow them to withdraw from the procedure altogether. In practice, most unsecured and hire purchase
creditors will *not* withdraw, whereas priority creditors
usually elect to withdraw from an order, preferring to
pursue their own sanction. This can cause problems if
you include, say, mortgage or rent arrears on your
administration order schedule, offer all your disposable
income on the form for distribution amongst creditors,
and then the building society or landlord decides to
withdraw from the order. So, if you have priority debts it
is best to negotiate them separately *before* you apply for
an administration order and use the administration
order procedure for your unsecured and hire purchase
debts only. Show arrangements for priority debts on
page 3 of Form N.92 and in your Financial Statement so
that it is clear to the court and your creditors that these
debts exist, that you are already dealing with them, and
that you are not asking the court to include them in the
administration order or to administer these debts.

When the Form N.92 has been filed at the court Office, the creditors scheduled to the administration order will be notified and a hearing date fixed.

You must attend at the hearing. Creditors may also attend, although in practice they rarely do. The hearing may be in open court or in chambers.

At the hearing the Registrar will consider the instalment offer you have made, and if he decides that you have offered a reasonable figure he will make the administration order. He can also at the same hearing consider whether it is appropriate to make an attachment of earnings order (see p. 188 above) to go with the administration order.

Once the administration order has been made, the creditor can theoretically use other enforcement procedures; in particular, he can apply for a warrant of execution against your goods, but *only* with the leave of the court after a court hearing of which you *must* be notified. It is extremely rare for a court to grant an application for a warrant *after* an administration order has been made and where the debtor is paying under the administration order.

Of course, if you fail to make payments under the administration order, the court can discharge (terminate) the order and you are back to a position where each creditor can enforce his debt against you separately.

If your circumstances change during the administration order period, you can apply to reduce or increase the payments.

Time orders

Under the Consumer Credit Act 1974, a borrower can apply to the county court for a time order, either before judgment but after a default notice has been served, or after judgment. He may apply in the case of both secured and unsecured loans, provided the loan agreements are 'regulated agreements' under the Act.

If you wish to apply for a time order, you must obtain from your local county court Office **Form N.440**, which asks for details of income and outgoings. File it at court with a Financial Statement, schedule of your other

Creditor/plaintiff issues default summons

Does debtor/defendant admit liability?

No — Consult a solicitor or law centre about possible defences

Yes — Fill in and send back to court form N.9

If form N.9 not filled in — Plaintiff requests judgment be entered — Order made for payment — Defendant can apply for administration order form N.92

Does plaintiff accept offer?

Yes — Judgment by consent — Order for payment by consent

No — Hearing — Registrar enters judgment and makes order for payment

Payment ordered in full or by instalments

Does defendant pay?

Yes — No further action (except possibly a charging order application)

No — **Has defendant applied for further time to pay or a reduction in instalments and new offer of payment (form N.245)?**

Yes

No

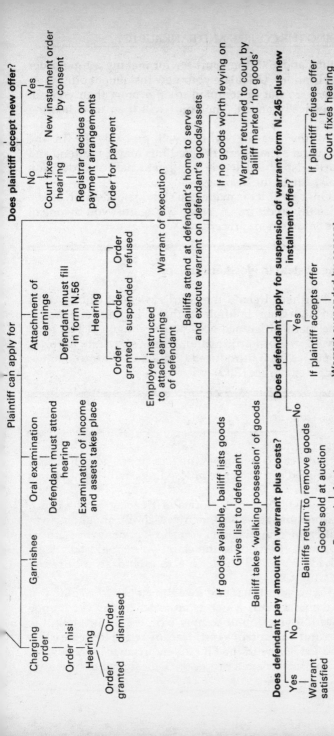

Chart 2. Default procedure in England and Wales

debts, and £30 (the court fee for making a time order application). Calculate your new instalment offer carefully – do not be tempted to offer more than you can realistically afford. The court will then fix a hearing date.

At the hearing, which will probably be in the Registrar's chambers, the creditors may also attend and the Registrar will decide whether to make an order. **You must attend the hearing.**

Once an order is made you should not default, otherwise the creditor may enforce it against you by one of the enforcement procedures set out above.

The System in Northern Ireland

In Northern Ireland the court system of county court and High Court is similar to that in England and Wales. The main difference occurs after judgment has been given. In Northern Ireland, a new system of enforcement has been introduced through the Enforcement of Judgment Office (EJO).

Unsecured debts

LESS THAN £300
An unsecured creditor suing for a debt of less than £300 is obliged to commence proceedings in the small claims court.

You will be sent a **Notice of Hearing** by the court, accompanied by a document which you should fill in to notify the court whether you admit or deny the claim. If you wish to dispute the claim you should take legal advice. You will then have to attend an arbitration hearing.

If you admit that you owe the money, the court will make an **award**, which is an order to pay the money owed. If you do not comply with the award, then the creditor will obtain a **certificate of award** from the court and lodge it with the EJO for enforcement (see below).

The small claims procedure is designed to be cheap,

quick and informal. Legal representation by either side is frowned upon.

DEBTS OVER £300

For debts over £300 the creditor will issue a **summons** through the court, which will be served on the defendant. The debtor will then be asked to indicate whether he disputes the claim.

If you wish to dispute the claim, take legal advice to ascertain whether you have a defence in law. If you do, the matter will proceed to trial. If you do not dispute the claim, the creditor will obtain a judgment for the amount owed.

Before any enforcement action can take place the creditor must register the judgment with the EJO.

After judgment has been given you can negotiate with the creditor on how the sum should be paid. If the creditor is anxious to avoid paying a substantial enforcement fee to the EJO, he may be prepared to accept any reasonable offer, calculated in accordance with the principles set out in Chapter 8.

However, if the debt remains outstanding and no agreement is reached, the creditor can apply to the EJO to enforce the debt. It is at this stage that the creditor will have to pay a fee to the EJO. The amount of the fee depends on the amount of the debt and is calculated on a sliding scale.

ENFORCEMENT THROUGH THE EJO

Normal procedure is for the EJO to call the debtor for an examination of means. If this course is followed, a **summons** will be issued for a hearing date. You should attend. If you cannot attend, owing to work or other commitments, inform the EJO, and an alternative date will be set. If you live a long way from the EJO it is possible for an officer of the EJO to visit you at home. If you do not cooperate with an examination of means, ultimately you can be arrested and brought before the court. The purpose of the examination is to find out about your income, outgoings and assets, so it is sensible to prepare a Financial Statement and a schedule of all your other debts to take to the hearing.

At the hearing the Registrar can make one of several orders:

- **An instalment order,** ordering the debtor to pay off the debt by monthly instalments.

- **Attachment of earnings order.** The EJO asks your employer for a statement of earnings and decides how much should be deducted from your wages or salary. An order is then issued to your employer with a copy to the creditor. In practice the EJO tends to make a *suspended* attachment order first to give you an opportunity of making the payments voluntarily; only if that fails will they actually send the order to your employer.

- **Order charging land.** If the EJO considers it appropriate, a creditor may be allowed to secure the debt upon the debtor's property (normally his house).

- **A notice of unenforceability.** If the EJO is satisfied that the debtor has no income or assets, it can declare that the debt is unenforceable. This means that the creditor can take no further action against you without the permission of the EJO.

- **Delivery of goods.** In certain cases where the court has given judgment for the delivery of goods to a creditor (for example in a hire purchase case), the EJO will issue a *notice of intention* to make an order for delivery of goods. This gives the debtor eight days to hand over the goods voluntarily. If the debtor does not hand over the goods, the EJO representative will attend at the debtor's home to enforce the order.

- **Seizure order.** The EJO does have the power to order the seizure of the debtor's assets in certain cirumstances. However, it is rarely used.

- **Committal proceedings.** If the debtor refuses to pay an instalment order made by the EJO, the creditor can commence proceedings to commit the debtor to prison for contempt of court. A debtor who finds he cannot comply with an instalment order due to a change in his circumstances should apply to the EJO for a variation of the instalment order (or an order of unenforceability if he can afford nothing) to avoid further proceedings. It is understood that committal proceedings are extremely rare.

The EJO in Northern Ireland operates a 'first past the post' system. The creditor who registers his judgment first takes priority over other unsecured creditors. This is unsatisfactory in terms of the principle of the fair distribution of disposable income as set out in Chapter 8. When dealing with the EJO it is most important that you explain that you have other debts and commitments. You should ensure that the EJO bears in mind your obligations to non-judgment creditors when deciding how to enforce a judgment on behalf of a creditor who has taken court proceedings.

On the other hand, creditors in Northern Ireland have criticised the EJO for being expensive and taking too long to produce results. This gives debtors an advantage in negotiation, since if creditors do not wish to use the ultimate sanction of court proceedings they are more likely to accept offers and to enter into negotiations.

The System in Scotland

In Scotland, debt cases are dealt with principally in the Sheriff's court and to a lesser extent in the higher Court of Session. The Sheriff's court also deals with criminal cases, so there is no separation of civil and criminal courts as in the English system.

Debt enforcement procedures in Scotland bear the general name of 'diligence', which is largely in the control of Sheriff's offices (similar to certificated bailiffs in England). The courts have far less control than in England, Wales and Northern Ireland.

Unsecured debts

In Scotland there are two separate procedures for the recovery of unsecured debts through the courts.

Debts of less than £1,000 are enforced by the issue of a summons in the Sheriff's court called **summary cause procedure**. Debts of over £1,000 are processed through either the Sheriff's court or the Court of Session by the issue of a writ called **ordinary cause procedure**.

SUMMARY CAUSE PROCEDURE

The creditor commences action by instructing a solicitor to issue a **summons** upon you. The creditor is called the pursuer and the debtor is called the defender. The papers you are sent will include a **Form Q**. You should fill in and return the form to the Sheriff's court before the return date, which is stated in the summons.

If you feel you may have a defence to the claim see a solicitor or seek some legal advice before completing the form. If you have no defence to the claim, check that the amount claimed by the pursuer is correct before making any admissions.

On the Form Q you have the opportunity to offer repayments by instalments. Calculate your offer in the way set out in Chapter 8. If the pursuer accepts your offer, you will not have to appear in court. If the pursuer does not accept your offer, there will be a court hearing on the **calling date**, when the Sheriff will decide whether your offer is reasonable or not. You can find out whether the pursuer has accepted your offer by telephoning the Sheriff's court on the day before the case calls. If there is to be a hearing before the Sheriff to decide whether your instalment offer is reasonable or not, take to the hearing a copy of your Financial Statement, a schedule of your other debts, showing how your offer to the pursuer has been calculated, and proof of your earnings if possible.

Once the court has made a **decree** that you owe the money claimed, you should commence making your instalments to the pursuer within seven days of the calling date. Instalment payments are paid directly to the pursuer and not through the court, so it is important to keep an accurate record of all the instalments you pay.

If you fail to fill in the Form Q by the return date, the pursuer can obtain a **decree in absence** seven days after the return date and proceed to **diligence**, that is, enforcement of the decree. By this time, court costs and interest will be added to the original debt. Normally simple interest is charged at the 'judicial rate of interest', which is presently 15 per cent per annum.

In the absence of an instalment arrangement, the pursuer can proceed to diligence 14 days after the Sheriff issues a decree. Similarly, if you default on your instalment payments, the pursuer can enforce the total amount of the decree plus interest and costs by diligence.

The pursuer obtains an **extract decree** from the Sheriff's court to prove that a decree has been granted and uses this to authorise the Sheriff's officers to commence diligence.

There are various enforcement options open to the Sheriff's officer:

Arrestment of wages

Before this can take place the Sheriff's officer will need to know the name and address of your employer. The arrestment is an instruction to your employer to freeze payment of your wages. Your employer must hold the wages until either you give permission for a distribution to proceed or the pursuer brings an action in the courts for **furthcoming** to get the money released. The money is distributed as follows:

- £4 to the employee

- 50% of surplus to the employee

- 50% of surplus to the arresting pursuer.

If a pursuer attempts to arrest your wages, you can often negotiate with the creditor to get more than £4 plus 50% released to you in return for authorising your employer to make a payment to the pursuer so that the pursuer can avoid the costs of bringing an action of furthcoming. Pursuers often use arrestment procedures in an attempt to persuade a debtor to enter into a regular instalment payment. Social security benefit and state pensions cannot be arrested.

Arrestment of other assets

Arrestment can also be used to freeze bank, building society or Post Office accounts, or money owed by a third party to the defender. In this case the person or organisation in possession of the money must release the money to the arresting pursuer or, in the case of one or more arresting pursuers, lodge the money in court so that the Sheriff can decide how it can be distributed.

Poinding and warrant sale

Poinding is where the Sheriff's officers visit your home to list property that could ultimately be sold to satisfy the unpaid decree.

The first warning that this procedure has been started is when you are served with a charge ordering you to pay the sum owed within 14 days. If you have not communicated with the pursuer/creditor previously, it is worth contacting him to see if you can make an arrangement for payment by instalments to avoid the poinding. Otherwise, if you do not pay the full amount within 14 days the Sheriff's officer will visit your home and poind goods up to the amount owed. Certain goods cannot be poinded, including:

- joint goods

- goods on hire purchase

- goods that do not belong to the debtor

- clothing

- essential furniture, i.e. beds, bedding materials, chairs and tables, items providing for heating, cooking, eating and storing food

● tools of your trade.

The officer also has to put a valuation on the property he poinds. If you think that the officer has poinded property that is exempt, or has undervalued property, it is possible to challenge the poinding by contacting the local Sheriff's Clerk immediately to complain. It is then advisable to seek advice from a money advisor, Citizens' Advice Bureau, law centre or solicitor.

In Scotland it is not an offence to remove property prior to poinding, but property cannot be removed from the home after the poinding has taken place and the list prepared.

Once the Sheriff's officer has valued and poinded the goods, if you do not offer to pay the debt or the value of the goods poinded, the Sheriff's officer can apply for a **warrant for sale**. However, a warrant should not be granted if the value of the poinded goods does not exceed the expenses of the proposed sale. The best way of preventing the warrant sale taking place is to find some defect in the poinding so that the case can be brought back before the Sheriff's court.

Once the warrant is granted, the sale is advertised and usually takes place in the defender's home by auction. To avoid the sale, negotiate with the Sheriff's officers to pay the debt by weekly instalments. Do not offer more than you can afford. Show the officers a copy of your Financial Statement to justify your offer. Contact the pursuer to explain to him that you wish now to make an offer.

ORDINARY CAUSE PROCEDURE

Ordinary cause procedure for debts over £1,000 is commenced in the Court of Session or the Sheriff's court by the creditor/pursuer issuing a writ. Enforcement procedures are similar to those for summary cause procedure except that there is no opportunity to offer payment by instalment. The enforcement procedures are normally carried out by the Sheriff's officer. If pursuers wish to use the additional enforcement procedure of **inhibition** – seeking to secure the decree on the defender's land and property (normally his house) – proceedings must be commenced in the Court of Sessions. If an inhibition is granted, it prevents the defender disposing of the property until the inhibition is removed. In practice, anyone purchasing property would check in the Register of Sassines in Edinburgh to see if an inhibition had been registered, and would probably expect the defender to arrange a bridging loan to pay off the inhibition before a sale of the property could take place.

PERSONAL BOND

Some creditors in Scotland invite a borrower to sign an agreement called a personal bond, which authorises the creditor to proceed straight to diligence through the Sheriff's officer if default occurs, and avoids the necessity of commencing proceedings through the Sheriff's court. You should consider very carefully your position before agreeing to sign such an agreement, since it allows the creditor to enforce the debt without any judicial interference at all.

Rates arrears

In Scotland, court proceedings for rates arrears take place in the Sheriff's court. The local collector of rates can apply to the Sheriff's court for a **summary warrant** to recover the arrears. When granted, the collector can recover the amount outstanding plus a 10 per cent additional charge. Once the summary warrant has been granted, the Sheriff's officer can be instructed immediately to enforce the debt by either **arrestment** or **poinding**. If the debt remains unpaid for more than four days after the poinding, a sale can take place after a further three days' notice to the debtor.

Imprisonment for rates arrears in Scotland still exists as a sanction, but is extremely rare. It can be ordered only where there has been a wilful non-payment, i.e. the debtor has the ability to pay but has refused. Imprisonment is for a maximum of six weeks.

Fines

Criminal proceedings in Scotland take place in the Sheriff's court. If found guilty of an offence it is open to the Sheriff to impose a fine. It is possible to make arrangements at the hearing to pay by instalments.

If you default on the ordered instalments you can be brought back to the Sheriff's court for a **means hearing**, where income and outgoings will be looked at and a decision made on whether to impose a sentence of imprisonment or whether to allow further time for payment.

If you are ordered to pay a fine by instalments and find that you cannot afford to make payments at the rate ordered, you should yourself apply to the Sheriff's Clerk for a means hearing for the matter to be re-considered.

Bankruptcy

Bankruptcy is a strategy that ultimately results in debts being written off. However, bankruptcy is a long, complicated, expensive and potentially traumatic experience for the debtor, who may have to endure considerable hardship, inconvenience and, in certain circumstances, unhappiness to achieve that outcome. Bankruptcy should thus be considered by most debtors only as an option of last resort, and not undertaken without the fullest legal and financial advice.

Bankruptcy proceedings are commenced by presentation of a **bankruptcy petition** to the Official Receiver's Office. Offices are situated in regional centres, whose address and telephone number will be found in the telephone directory under 'Official Receiver in Bankruptcy'. A debtor can present his own petition on payment of a fee, which is presently in excess of £100. A creditor can also petition for a debtor's bankruptcy, but will have to pay a larger fee, presently in excess of £200. Under the provisions of the Insolvency Act 1985, a creditor's petition can be presented where the debt or debts of the presenting creditor or creditors amount to more than £750.

The bankruptcy procedure may involve a **public examination** at which the debtor will be cross-examined about his assets, debts and the reasons for his bankruptcy.

Here are a few points to bear in mind when considering this option:

* If adjudged bankrupt, the debtor will become a financial 'non-person', since a trustee in bankruptcy is appointed to take control of all the bankrupt's assets.

* It is extremely difficult for an undischarged bankrupt to operate a bank account.

* A bankrupt cannot become a director of a limited company.

* A bankrupt cannot have credit in excess of a statutory amount (presently £50) without informing the potential creditor that he is an undischarged bankrupt.

* It is extremely difficult for an undischarged bankrupt to carry on any trade or business on his own account.

* Many professions disqualify bankrupts from practising while they are bankrupt.

* Some public offices are closed to bankrupts, e.g. a bankrupt cannot be a magistrate.

* The family home, if owned totally or partially by the bankrupt, becomes a realisable asset in the bankruptcy.

* The administrative costs of a bankruptcy are considerable, and all the assets may be exhausted in meeting the costs, leaving no money to pay the actual creditors.

* If the bankrupt inherits any property during the period of the bankruptcy, this will become an asset in the bankruptcy.

* Some fuel boards will not allow a bankrupt to have fuel on credit. The bankrupt will either have to pay by slot

meter, weekly or monthly payments, or have the supply
connected in the spouse's name, or face disconnection.

* During the bankruptcy period the bankrupt may be
asked by his trustee to make payments from income to
the trustee for distribution to the creditors.

Discharge from bankruptcy

A bankrupt can apply for discharge from bankruptcy at
any time after he has been adjudged bankrupt, but an
automatic application for discharge is presented after
three years, or five years in certain circumstances. The
court will then consider whether to allow the bankrupt
to be discharged and will consider whether to enter
judgment for a proportion of the outstanding debts
after discharge.

It is only after the bankrupt has been discharged that
he becomes free of the debts, subject of course to any
judgment that the court may impose on him for a
proportion of the bankruptcy debts.

Since the Insolvency Act 1985, bankruptcy has become a slightly more attractive option for debtors with
large debts, since a measure of protection is now given
to the bankrupt's household goods. It is most *attractive*
for debtors who are not working and are not likely to
work again, who are tenants and have no wish to be
owner-occupiers, and who are not very concerned
about their credit rating.

It is most *unattractive* for debtors who are self-
employed, who are owner-occupiers, and who hope to
be able to use the cheaper forms of credit in the future,
and for those who are likely to inherit property during
the bankruptcy period.

Conclusion

Each of the three court systems in England and Wales,
Scotland and Northern Ireland has its special features
and problems. All of them need to be taken very
seriously by the debtor. The Scottish procedure of

arrestment of earnings, in particular, can be very harmful to someone struggling to cope with financial problems.

All the systems, however, have one major fault: they are based on individual actions in the courts by individual creditors. The courts therefore have to attempt to make a fair judgment of the circumstances as regards each different debt rather than of the overall circumstances of the debtor and the need to pay *all* creditors. This is why it is absolutely essential for a court to know your full position if you have a number of credit and other (e.g. rates) commitments. In our view, in the best of worlds any action for debt should automatically result in the court requiring such information to be forthcoming, as they seek to do in Northern Ireland. The importance of having your Financial Statement ready for every court case you may face is thus clear. If you are unlucky enough to end up in the courts, the outcome will depend on the quality, accuracy and logic of the information you provide about your *whole* situation.

10

The Need for Reform

In this book we have shown consumers how to get the best credit deals available to them and cope with any indebtedness they may have. To do this we have explained the complex calculations, laws, rules, procedures and attitudes that are involved both for credit-users and credit-granters. We hope this book will help you, the reader, with your own money worries or those of your friends and relatives. We expect, in practice, it will not be all that easy to work things through. What we now want to do is to suggest how it could be made easier to deal with debt.

Changing the Atmosphere

The money-lending market has developed and expanded rapidly, not only amongst the higher-income groups, but also in the lower-income groups, which are often more vulnerable to default owing to lower incomes, tighter budgets and less job security. This development appears to have been positively encouraged by government policy through deregulation of credit restrictions. In a society so dependent upon credit to sell its products, it is therefore inefficient that there is such a clumsy and involved system for dealing with the small, if rising, percentage of borrowers who default. It is also hypocritical to adopt attitudes to default rooted in the values of an age when borrowing was a dubious practice at best for all but the rich.

This judgemental approach is found in the following small but significant example. A major firm of bailiffs has an office near the court. Many people go here to pay money when they receive a notice from the bailiffs. These are fraught and unhappy circumstances for the debtor, who has often borrowed the money to pay, or is using money for this debt that he needs for others. This situation is not the bailiffs' fault, but the bailiffs seem to rub in the debtors' distress by the way in which they receive them at their offices. In this case the debtor must enter a tiny reception office (cubicle would be a better word) through a barred door. There is no seating, room only for five or six people (it is often crowded), and just a hatch with a very small opening in it through which to talk to the receptionist. There is no privacy at all. Everyone can see and overhear everything. This is humiliating and belies the goodwill of a company that says it is as sympathetic to debtors as its job allows it to be. This same firm nevertheless found the money to install an expensive and highly sophisticated main-frame computer system to deal with the number of accounts it administers. Could it not also have improved its reception office to give some dignity and privacy to those whose money it, in effect, relies on?

Given these kinds of problems, it is not surprising that borrowers experience so much fear, mistrust and anxiety in their dealings with creditors and debt collectors. There is a clear connection between our ownership of money and credit-worthiness and our personal status and esteem, between our ability to gratify our wishes and our sense of security. Money has a symbolic importance, and the feelings that are aroused when we know we are threatened in some way as a result of a lack of it go some way to explain why debtors are reluctant to communicate with creditors and why creditors are so emotional about default. There is a real case for further psychological and social study in this important area because at present we tend to see money problems as the result of other difficulties rather than as the *cause* of the difficulty.

To enable borrowers to become more open with creditors about their true circumstances, a different approach to default and collection is needed.

A New Approach to Default

A national money advice service

A neutral and independent debt advice service, of the kind pioneered at Birmingham Settlement Money Advice Centre, ought to be available to debtors. If a national body such as the Money Advice Association were able to set up a national money advice and debt counselling service to ensure that the best and most pragmatic arrangements in each individual case were made between a debtor and his creditors, this could only greatly enhance the chance of limiting the costs of default and the stigma and fear involved. Such a national money advice service could be funded, we believe, by a levy of perhaps 0.5 per cent on the turn-over of credit companies as related to personal borrowing. Central government and local government ought also to contribute to help those who, by reason of their poverty, are involved not in consumer credit but in rent, rates, fuel and water rates arrears. Banks and building societies should also be required to contribute. Almost all bodies concerned with debt, from the Office of Fair Trading to the National Consumer Council and the National Association of Citizens' Advice Bureaux, believe such a service is necessary.

A national borrowers' league

Individuals with consumer credit commitments might be invited to subscribe as members to a league charged with the duty to protect the legitimate interests of borrowers. There are already many associations that protect the interests of creditors. The government might give some launch funds to prime such an initiative if only because one result of society's reliance upon consumer spending to boost the economy is the need to protect borrowers' interests. Such a league could then:

- represent borrowers in national debates on credit and debt and make representation to institutions concerned with such matters,

- organise better insurance for borrowers against un-expected short-term default,

- act as a channel of communication between borrowers and creditors and institutions concerned with both on issues and problems that arise,

- work to ensure the maximum education of borrowers on matters of credit and debt.

Improvements in creditors' procedures
The development of a national money advice service and a borrowers' league, however, will take time. In the meantime we invite credit-granters and debt collectors to look at their default and collection procedures urgently to see:

- whether they are sensitive in their dealings with de-faulters and whether negotiations are conducted in privacy and by polite and understanding members of their staff;

- whether their systems actually encourage defaulters to communicate with them – defaulters often complain that they do not communicate because it simply makes things worse;

- that attempts are made to establish personal contact to find the real reason for the default – creditors could then ensure that all subsequent action acknowledged the realities of the situation;

- whether their procedures are capable of revision to meet different circumstances when the real cause of default is known – this would, we believe, mean intro-ducing modified recovery arrangements earlier than is now the case, thus avoiding expensive recourse to the courts;

- whether they can put up notices in their offices and/or mail simple leaflets with their letters to defaulters explaining the need to get in touch, examining the options open to the defaulter and telling the defaulter where to go for money advice if it is needed;

- whether they can consult with each other through their various national associations about how best to promote the establishment of a national debt counselling and money advice service.

Credit-granters must understand that if they support the pledging of part of future incomes to themselves from groups more vulnerable to changes in their circumstances, or made so by the amount of credit they are granted, they have to deal with default on the basis that they have a duty to help a client *all* the way through a difficult patch. Equally, borrowers must make sure their credit-granters are not neglected and are kept informed.

Poverty and Debt

Debt and default are very much an experience of people who fall into poverty, or whose incomes are generally too low, or too variable, to make them good risks for credit-granters except at very high rates of interest. We feel that society ought to do more to help those in poverty move out of the cycle of debt and deprivation it represents. This would involve developing a means whereby the cycle of poverty could be broken, and this means more money for the relief of poverty, not less. We had hoped that the current review of the social security system might provide a means whereby such changes could be achieved, but we fear that the legislative proposals will worsen rather than improve the position of people living in poverty.

In the absence of an improved system, there is a real

need for poorer people to be able to use credit on terms appropriate to their situation. **Credit unions** seem to us to offer the best hope for this and ought to be widely encouraged. The suppliers of goods and services might well be persuaded to develop new relationships with the Association of British Credit Unions to help credit unions grow and develop nationally. Local authorities that are investing resources in the development of credit unions are much to be commended.

A more radical approach would be for central government to set up a system of interest-free loans for the lower-income groups, not as part of the social security system to replace entitlement to state benefits, but as additional assistance. This could be done through a **people's bank** specially created for the purpose.

Loans from credit unions or interest free from a people's bank are unlikely to help those most deeply in debt, however, and other measures are needed to improve their position and enable them to re-establish themselves within society. For example:

* Imprisonment for civil debt should be abolished. Imprisonment is a criminal sanction and as such is inappropriate for a civil matter.

* Disconnection of electricity, gas and water supplies should be a sanction of last resort and permissible only by order of an independent arbitrator, after all the facts and alternative options have been considered.

* In the case of mortgage or secured loan arrears, a code of practice should be established that lenders would be obliged to follow *prior* to commencing court proceedings. The code would require other options to be explored with the borrower as an alternative to loss of home. The courts should be given greater powers to make postponed or suspended orders so that the borrower's home could be preserved in times of temporary financial difficulty.

* where repossession of a house took place, the lender should be under a duty to obtain the best price, and

would be given a reasonable length of time in which to sell the property, after which no further monthly payments could be charged to the borrower's account.

Reform of the Courts

In addition to the above, the courts in the United Kingdom are in need of radical reform so that the system attains the following objectives:

- to distinguish between those who *cannot* pay their debts and those who *will not* pay,

- to provide both creditor and debtor with information and advice concerning their rights within the system,

- to make the courts equally accessible to both creditor and debtor,

- to acknowledge the debtor's obligations to his dependants and his rights to the basic essentials of life,

- to achieve a fair balance between the claims of competing creditors,

- to facilitate the rehabilitation of debtors and their return to a normal participation in the economy.

At the moment, the courts are seen as places of calamity rather than the forum for fair-minded arbitration. There is confusion in the public mind as to their criminal and civil functions. The system is seen as unfair because creditors as plaintiffs are advised and represented by lawyers who are accustomed to using the courts, thus putting the unrepresented debtor at a disadvantage – not knowing when to speak, whom to speak to and what to say. The courts need to be seen as accessible and fair to all: legal paraphernalia needs to be dismantled, and plain English introduced into court forms.

There is an argument for ceasing to use the term

'courts' at all. It would be helpful if another name could be found that clearly explains, as the present names do not, the functions of the county court and Sheriff's court in Scotland.

In every civil court there should be a welfare officer plus support staff, to whom the Registrar could refer an unrepresented defendant for independent advice and assistance concerning his case. There is only one such officer in the country at the present time in the Birmingham County Court. This seems to us to be a model that should be widely copied in the interests of achieving the courts' aim of fair adjudication upon a question.

Rehabilitation of the debtor, even where this means writing off all or part of the debt, is an essential component of any new system. Bankrupts can now obtain a discharge of their debts after three years. We believe that a similar release should be granted to the ordinary judgment debtor, possibly through reform of the administration order procedure, so that after regular payment over a fixed period of time the debtor could be free of debt and return once again to normal participation in the economic system.

Responsible Lending

More also needs to be done in the areas of debt prevention and responsible lending:

* Creditors should be scrupulous in their choice of third parties through whom to supply credit,

* Secured loans be given only where the credit-granter is quite satisfied that the borrower understands that if default occurs the home will be repossessed,

* Secured loans should be given only where the borrower has received independent advice on the disadvantages and consequences of default,

* Mortgages should be granted only after pre-purchase advice on the disadvantages of home ownership as well as the advantages.

A national credit register
The credit industry has recently called for the establishment of a national credit register where each individual credit-user would be registered with details of each credit commitment. Credit-granters see this as advantageous because they could check on a borrower's pre-existing commitments before deciding to advance new credit, and they claim that this would enable them to lend more responsibly.

If such a register were administered independently of the credit industry it could have a wider use with advantages for others besides the credit industry. Borrowers could receive a computer print-out showing their overall indebtedness, rather than individual notices from each creditor. The courts could use the register to assist in establishing whether a particular defendant had other credit commitments that the court needed to take into account. Steps would have to be taken to ensure confidential details of borrowers' finances did not fall into the wrong hands, and to ensure that credit-granters did not use the information for marketing or canvassing purposes. With these safeguards, the register could have a valuable part to play in the overall package of reforms.

The credit society is here to stay for the foreseeable future. The recent recession, coupled with the huge growth in credit, has produced a crisis – perhaps not yet a crisis for the credit industry, with its large profits to sustain it, but many individual personal crises all over the country. Debt is now a possibility for most of us, a probability for some of us, and an inevitability for a small but growing percentage of the poorest members of society.

The way we grant credit and the way in which default is handled must change. Attitudes to debt must improve. We believe that the reforms we have suggested will go a long way to achieving these changes, and look forward to participating in the continuing debate that we hope this book will encourage.

Self-Help Kit

YOUR PERSONAL BUDGET

NET INCOME

	Weekly	Monthly
Wages/salary – yours		
Wages/salary – your partner's		
FIS		
Child Benefit		
Unemployment Benefit		
Supplementary Benefit		
Disability Benefit		
Retirement Pension		
Other pension		
Sickness Benefit		
Maintenance		
Non-dependant contributions	___	___
Total income	===	===

	Weekly	Monthly	Annually
Overtime YES/NO	___	___	___
TOTAL	===	===	===

REGULAR OUTGOINGS

	Weekly	Monthly
Mortgage/rent		
2nd mortgage		
Rates		
Water rates		
Ground rent		
Service charge		
Life insurance		
House insurance		
Electricity		
Gas		
Oil		
Coal		
Housekeeping		
School meals		
Pocket money (children)		
Travelling to work*		
Travelling to school		
Telephone		
TV rental		
TV licence		
Newspapers		
Cigarettes		
Entertainment		
Maintenance		
Childminding/nursery		
Regular prescriptions		
Laundry/launderette		
Fines		
Other (1)		
(2)		
(3)		
(4)		
Total		
Credit commitments (1)		
(2)		
(3)		
(4)		
(5)		
(6)		
Total		

Page 2

IRREGULAR OUTGOINGS

	Weekly	*Monthly*
Clothing		
Christmas		
Birthdays		
Extra school expenses		
Toys and books		
Repairs		
Replacements		
Decoration		
Holidays		
Subscriptions		
Prescriptions (health expenses)		
Sporting activities		
Hobbies	_____	_____
Total	══════	══════
Add regular outgoings	_____	_____
Total outgoings	══════	══════

Now compare your total outgoings with your
   total income:

Income		
Less total outgoings	_____	_____
Balance	══════	══════

Page 3

---

* If travel is by car, include: petrol ⎫
                             tax ⎬ averaged on a weekly/monthly
                       insurance ⎬ basis
                       servicing ⎭

YOUR FINANCIAL STATEMENT

PART I – YOUR INCOME

Income (net)   *Weekly*   *Monthly*
Wages/salary – (1)
Wages/salary – (2)
Housing Benefit
Child Benefit
Family Income Supplement
Unemployment Benefit
Disability/Invalidity Benefit
Sickness Benefit
Supplementary Benefit
Retirement Pension
Any other pensions or benefit
Maintenance
Contributions from non-dependant
Irregular overtime
Part-time earnings – (1)
                – (2)

Any other income

Total income

PART II – YOUR OUTGOINGS

Category 1 – Essential	Weekly	Monthly
Mortgage/rent		
2nd mortgage		
Rates		
Water rates		
Ground rent		
Gas		
Electricity		
Other fuel		
Housekeeping		
Life insurance		
House insurance		
School meals		
Pocket money		
Child minding/nursery		
Travelling expenses		
Fines		
Maintenance		
TV rental		
TV licence		
Laundry or launderette	___	___
Total	═══	═══
Total income		
Less Category 1 outgoings	___	___
Balance	═══	═══

Category 2 – Essential items hard to quantify	*Weekly*	*Monthly*
Clothing/shoes		
School expenses (not meals)		
Books and toys		
Repairs to property		
Replacement of or repairs to essential household items		
Redecoration		
Health expenses (dental, prescriptions, opticians)		
Entertainment, birthdays, Christmas		
Total	___	___
Add Category 1 outgoings	___	___
Total essential outgoings	___	___
Total income		
Less total essential outgoings		
Balance	___	___

Category 3 – Non-essential	*Weekly*	*Monthly*
Cigarettes/alcohol (see p. 116)		
Gambling/bingo		
Holidays		
Video rental		
Meals out		
Subscriptions to clubs, etc.		
Sporting activities		
Telephone (see p. 117)		
Hobbies		
Any other	_____	_____
Total	======	======
Add Category 1 and 2 outgoings	_____	_____
Total outgoings	======	======
Total income		
Less total outgoings	_____	_____
Disposable income	======	======

You may now need to go through your Category 3 and even Category 2
expenditure to bring your budget into balance. If you have too little
money to do this, you must let the figures speak for themselves in any
court.

PART III – YOUR ARREARS

Priority debts	*Weekly*	*Monthly*
Mortgage/rent		
2nd mortgage/secured loan		
Rates		
Water rates		
Gas		
Electricity		
Fines		
Maintenance		
Income tax		
VAT		
HP (less than ⅓ paid)		
Total		

Once priority debt payments have been agreed with your creditors, they can be included with your normal outgoings.

	Weekly	Monthly
Disposable income		
Less priority debt payments		
Final disposable income		

Remaining debts		
Unsecured loans		
HP		
Credit card		
Charge card		
Catalogue		
Other		
Total		

Final disposable income		
Less remaining debts		

If your final disposable income is insufficient to pay off your remaining debts, you *must* offer payments to your creditors on the basis of the system described in Chapter 8.

Further Reading

The Credit Book by Adrienne Gleeson (Kogan Page, 1985).

The National Consumer Council Reports – Consumers in Debt, Consumers & Credit and the Consumers in Debt Conference reports.

Disability Rights Handbook (Disability Alliance, 25 Denmark Street, London WC2).

Divorce – Legal Procedures and Financial Facts (Consumers' Association, 1984).

National Welfare Benefits Handbook by Ruth Cohen and Beth Lakhani (Child Poverty Action Group, 1 Macklin Street, London WC2B 5NH; new edition each year).

Rights Guide to Non Means Tested Social Security Benefits by Ruth Cohen and Beth Lakhani (Child Poverty Action Group, 1 Macklin Street, London WC2B 5NH; new edition each year).

Fuel Rights Handbook (SHAC/WRUG, 1985; available from London Housing Aid Centre, 189A Old Brompton Road, London SW5).

Rights Guide for Home Owners by Jo Tunnad and Clare Whately (CPAG/SHAC, 1985, 1 Macklin Street, London WC2B 5NH).

Taxation Simplified by A. H. Taylor (Lofthouse Publications; new edition each year).

Making the Most of Your Money by Louise Botting and Vincent Duggleby (Orbis Publishing, 1985).

County Court Procedures by John Blamire (Birmingham Settlement Money Advice Centre, 318 Summer Lane, Birmingham B19 3RL, 1983).

Dealing with Debt by John Blamire (Birmingham Settlement Money Advice Centre, 318 Summer Lane, Birmingham B19 3RL, 1984).

Sales – The Law Relating to Bankruptcy, Liquidation and Receivership by J. H. Thompson (Macdonald Evans, 1977).

Debts under £1,000 (Castlemilk Law Centre, 30 Dougrie Drive, Glasgow G45 9AD, 1986). For Scottish readers.

How to Split up – and Survive Financially by A. Hetherington (Allen & Unwin, 1986).

The Office of Fair Trading also publish a number of booklets on the Consumer Credit Act and its operation.

Index

ACAS 83
Administration of Justice Act 58
Administration Orders 190, 191
  how to apply 190
  costs of 190
Advertising 72
  of credit 40, 72
Alcohol 104, 116
Annual Percentage Rate
  APR 20, 22–32, 33, 38, 39, 46
  definition of 19
Arrestment of Wages (Scotland) 201, 202
Association of British Credit Unions 46, 214
Attachment of Earnings 95, 188, 189, 193
  protected earnings level 189

Bailiffs 123, 182, 187, 188, 192, 195, 210
  and Rent arrears 132, 182
  and Rates arrears 133, 134, 182
  and Eviction 139, 182
  rights of 187
  Walking possession by 187, 195
  costs of 132, 188, 195
Bankruptcy 205–8, 216
  definition of 205
  petition 205
  Official Receiver 205
  trustee in 206, 207
  public examination 206
  discharge from 207
Banks 1, 21, 22, 23, 124, 182, 211
  credit offered by 21, 27
  credit cards of 22, 23
  peoples 214
Benefit Books
  taking away of 43

Benefits
  see Housing Benefit
  see Supplementary Benefit
  see FIS
  living on 87, 119
Bingo 116
Birmingham Settlement Money Advice Centre 10, 14, 15, 60, 104, 177, 211
Black Economy 99–100
Borrowers League 211
Borrowing 72, 73
  as a possible solution to debt 72, 73, 129
  from friends and relatives 73, 74, 97, 101
Building Society Account
  as a way of budgeting 114

Catalogues 24
Charge Cards 24
Charging Order Act 189
Charging Orders 189, 192
  definition of 189
  effect of 189
Charities 96, 97, 101
Chartered Accountant 94
  when to consult 81
  priority debt and 147
Check Trading 26
Child Benefit 79, 90
  One Parent Benefit
Child Poverty Action Group 90
Cigarettes 65, 96, 104, 115, 116
Citizens Advice Bureau 43, 52, 73, 84, 85, 90, 96, 128, 147, 168, 177, 203
Clothing 67, 68
  as essential outgoing 67, 104, 112, 113

Consolidated Loan Plan 72
Consumer Advice Centre 43, 73, 177
Consumer Credit Association 60
Consumer Services Department 60
County Court 2, 136, 144, 153, 154, 158, 179, 186–7, 190, 192, 193, 272
    default proceedings 179
    possession proceedings 179
    Possession Summons 179
    Welfare Officer in 216
Court Forms
    Forms Q 200, 201
    responding to 179, 180
    N.9 184, 194
    N.10 183
    N.11 180
    N.56 188
    N.92 190, 192, 193, 194
    N.245 186, 194, 195
    N.445 193
Court Orders 130, 131
    Attachment of Earnings 95, 188, 189, 193
    Changing Order 189, 195
    garnishee Order 190, 193
    Instalment Orders 188, 189, 194
    Oral Examination 186, 195
    Suspended Order 188, 189
    Time Orders 193
    variation of 189
Court proceedings 77, 123, 145, 175
    adjournment of 180, 181
    commital 198, 199
    costs of 175, 177
    default summons 184
    disadvantages for creditors 125–6
    financial statement and 145, 180, 183, 185, 186, 189, 190
    fixed date Summons 182–3
    for fines 132, 133, 134, 205
    for HP arrears 123, 146, 182, 183

    for mortgage arrears 121, 179, 181, 182
    for rate arrears 133, 134, 204
    for rent arrears 130, 131, 179, 181
    in Chambers 178
    in Northern Ireland 196–9
    in Open Court 178
    in Scotland 199–205
    Legal Aid in 177, 180
    Oral Examination 186
    particulars of claim and 184
    responding to 176
    Time Orders 193
    Warrant of Execution 187, 193, 194
    Warrant of Possession 182
    Warrant of Recovery 183
Courts 94, 95, 110, 129, 215
    see Court proceedings 175 on-wards
    see County Court
    see High Court
    see Court System – Scotland
    see Court System – Northern Ireland
    attending at 128
    contempt of 199
    feelings about 176, 177
    Legal Aid in 177, 180, 184
    offers to 181, 184, 185
    personnel in 178, 179
    Registrars 216
Court System – in Northern Ireland 196–9
    Certificate of Award 196
    commital proceedings 198, 199
    delivery of goods 198
    Enforcement of Judgment Office 196–9
    Examination of means 197
    Notice of Hearing 196
    Notice of Unenforceability 198
    Order changing land 198
    Registering a Judgment 197
    Seizure Order 198
    Summons 197

Court System – in Scotland 199–205
  arrestment of wages 201, 202
  arrestment of other assets 202
  calling date 200
  Court of Session 199, 200, 203, 204
  decree 200
  diligence 199, 201
  Ordinary Cause procedure 200, 203, 204
  poinding 202, 203
  Sheriffs Court 199, 200, 201, 203, 204, 205, 217
  Sheriffs Office 199, 201, 202, 204
  Summary Cause proceedings 200, 203
  Warrant Sale 202, 203
Credit 62, 65, 104, 119, 209, 211, 212, 214, 217
  advertising of 18–19
  Credit Black list 167, 170
  Credit Brokers 27
  consequences of reducing payment 170
  costs of 28
  definition of 18, 19
  early settlement of 42, 73
  in shops 23
  interest free 23
  Instant 24
  revolving 20, 32
  Secured 21, 30, 72
  types of 20–7
  Unsecured 21, 30
Credit Agreement 40–5
  cancellability of 41, 42
  contents of 40
  duty to provide information 43
  guaranteeing 44
  obtaining copies 152
  statutory provisions 40
  termination of 49, 50
Credit Cards 22, 23, 24, 53
  interest on 23
  return of 158

Credit Granter (see also creditor) 72, 146, 209, 213, 217
  branch office of 54
  communication with 61
  complaints about 60
  Head Office of 53
  harassment 58, 59, 60, 61
  licensing of 33, 39
  registration of 33, 72
  visits from 55
Credit Rating 170
Credit Reference Agency 37
Credit Sale agreement 25
  consequences of reducing payment 170
Credit Unions
  advantages of 45, 46, 214
  operation of 45
Credit Worthiness 2
Creditor (see also Credit Granter) 107, 108, 114, 116, 117, 118, 147, 150, 210
  accepting offers 162, 163
  and Court proceedings 18, 57, 58, 176, 177
  communications with 61, 76, 77, 117, 121, 122, 149, 161, 162
  Financial Statement and 77, 106, 122, 156, 159, 162
  improving procedure 61, 212, 213, 216
  negotiations with 77, 156
  refusing offers 162, 163, 166
Customs and Excise 147

Death 34, 45, 173
Debt 1–17, 62, 71, 72, 75, 76, 77, 84, 86, 103, 104, 105, 117, 120, 121, 122, 123, 134, 217
  and poverty 213
  blame for 16, 17
  causes of 3–5, 84, 86
  experience of 9–16
  onset of 1, 2, 3
  to friends and relatives 73, 74, 174
  writing off 172, 173

Debt Collector 53, 56, 57, 150
    complaints about 60
Default 48, 49, 50, 51, 60, 61, 133,
        143, 209, 211, 212, 213
    creditors attitude to 48, 209, 210
    creditors rights on 49
    interest 49
    service charges and 152
Default notice 49, 143
    contents of 50
Default Summons 184
Defective goods 154, 155
Delivery of goods (Northern
        Ireland) 198
DHSS 84, 86, 88, 90, 99, 100, 109,
        131, 136, 139, 141
    National Insurance contribu-
        tions 64, 99, 147
    direct payments by 86, 95
Diligence (Scotland) 199, 201
Director-General of Fair Trading
        153
Disposable Income 103, 131, 133,
        147, 156, 171
    calculation of 118, 149, 156
    when none exists 149, 171
Distraint
    and rates arrears 123, 142
    and rent arrears 123, 131, 132
Divorce 93, 94, 96, 100
Door-to-door collection 53, 56, 150

Earnings
    see also wages 63, 79, 81, 83, 94,
        96
    increasing 84
    part-time 84, 85
    casual/black economy 99,100
Education grants 97, 98
Electricity
    see fuel 109, 123, 139, 214
Electricity Consultative Council
        137
Equity 124, 125
Essential outgoings 76, 103, 110,
        114, 142

    see also expenditure
    categories of 104, 105
    housekeeping as 106, 107, 112
Eviction 96, 182
    and rent arrears 123, 130, 182
    and mortgage arrears 123, 182
    warrant of possession and 182
Examination of means (Northern
        Ireland) 197
Expenditure 62, 73, 76, 77, 103
    irregular definition of 67, 68
    regular definition of 65
    categories of 104, 110, 112, 113,
        115, 118, 119
Extortionate Credit 40, 42

Fair Trading
    Director-General of 153
    Office of 6, 33, 37, 39, 47, 57
Family Income Supplement FIS 86,
        100, 125
    and low wages 83, 86
    definition of 86
    how to claim 86
Finance Company 75, 124
    Branch office 53, 54
    Head office 53
Financial Statement 76, 78, 100,
        101, 102, 116, 120, 146, 147
    administration orders 190
    casual earnings 100
    Court proceedings 77, 143, 144,
        180
    essential outgoings 103, 104,
        106, 110, 112, 114
    Fines 110, 143
    income maximisation 78
    importance of 77, 78, 120, 121-2
    maintenance arrears 145
    mortgage arrears 125, 130, 183
    priority debt 121, 149, 156, 185
    rates arrears 133, 134, 135, 183
    rent arrears 131, 132, 183
    secured debts 156
    unsecured debts 156, 159, 185

Fines 142
    as an essential outgoing 105,
        110, 123
    administration orders 192
    Court appearance for 123, 205
    Financial Statement 110, 143
    imprisonment and 110, 123, 143,
        205
    in Scotland 205
    payment of 110, 143, 144
    reduction of 110, 143, 144
Free prescriptions 88, 113
Free school meals 88
Fuel 65, 75, 88, 91, 104, 105, 109
    Administration Orders 192
    Budget Schemes 109
    Code of Practice 136
    Direct Payments 141
    DHSS and 88
    disconnections 136
    how to pay 109, 110, 137
    sanctions for debt 136
    Savings Stamps 109
    slot meter 109, 137
    token meters 140

Gambling 104, 116
Garnishee
    proceedings 189
    Orders 190
Gas
    see fuel 109, 123, 240
Gas Consumer Council 137

Harassment 44, 58, 59, 60, 61
    by creditors 60, 130
    of debtors 58, 59, 60, 130
High Court 144, 178, 179, 190
    service of writ 179
    time limits in 179
Hire Purchase 88, 108
    Administration Orders 190, 191,
        192, 193
    as priority debt 123, 146
    Court proceedings 123, 146, 182,
        183

creditor terminates agreement
    50
default on 50, 51, 52
definition of 25
final sanction 123
hirer terminates agreement 51
repossession of goods 146, 187,
    188
one-third rule 123, 146, 183
Holidays 68, 117
Homelessness
    and mortgage arrears 128
Housing Aid Centre 128
Housing Associations 128
Housing Benefit 86, 87, 100
    backdating of 130
    low wages 83
    owner-occupiers and 87
    rates arrears 133
    rent arrears 131
    rent rebate 130
    tenants and 87, 130

Imprisonment
    abolition of 214
    fines arrears 110
    Income Tax 123
    maintenance arrears 123
    ·rates arrears 123, 204
Income Support 89
    replacing Supplementary Ben-
        efit 89
Income Tax 4, 64, 79, 81, 94, 95, 147
    allowances 79, 82
    coding 80, 81
    covenants 98
    Imprisonment 123
    lodgers 91
    PAYE 79
    separation and divorce 93, 94
    separate assessment 82
    single parents 82
    unmarried/cohabiting 82, 94
    unemployed 82
Inland Revenue 79, 80, 91, 147
    leaflets 82

phone-in 82
Insurance 65
  as an essential outgoing 105, 107
  credit insurance 39, 47
  house contents insurance 105,
    107
  house insurance 105, 107
  insurance policies 75, 97
Interest 72, 80, 126
  effects of Judgment on 166
  extortionate 40–2, 154
  freezing of 158, 163
  judicial rate of (Scotland) 201
  rates of 72, 124
  repayment programmes 126,
    159
  suspension of 158, 163
Irregular expenditure 67–8, 114

Job Centre 12
Joint and Several liability 44
Joint liability 44

Law Centre 91
Legal Aid 177, 180
  Green Form Scheme 177
  for Court Representation 180
  solicitors 91, 145, 180
Licensing
  of credit grantors 33, 39
  revocation of licence 39
  Road Fund Licence 107
Loan Sharks 43, 44
Loans – Secured 65, 72, 73, 216
  Unsecured 21, 72, 73
  from relatives and friends 73, 74,
    97, 101
Lodgers 90, 91, 101
  income from 90, 91
Low Wages 79, 82, 83, 84, 86

Mail Order 24
Maintenance 94, 95, 106, 110, 114,
    128
  arrears 123, 145

Court proceedings 145
Financial Statement 145
increasing 95
irregular 94, 95, 100
reducing 95
Misrepresentation 155
Mortgage
  see also second mortgage 65, 91,
    105, 125, 217
  deed 124
  definition of 123, 124
  how to pay 109
  income tax 80, 125
  interest on 87, 125, 126
  lodgers 91
  re-mortgage 127
Mortgage arrears 121, 123, 124,
    128–9
  Administration Order 190, 191
  borrowing to pay off 129, 72–3
  capitalisation of 126
  Court proceedings 124, 177, 181,
    182
  eviction 182
  possession summons 179
  sanctions for 123
  warrant of possession 182
MIRAS 80, 125

National   Borrowers   League
    211–12
National Consumer Council 211
National Credit Register 217
National Insurance Contributions
    64, 81, 99, 147
NSPCC 9
Non-dependent 91, 92–3
  contributions of 91, 92, 93, 101
Notice   of   unenforceability
    (Northern Ireland) 198

Office of Fair Trading 6, 33, 37, 39,
    47, 57, 211
Official Receiver 205
Oral Examination 186
Over-commitment 7–8

Overtime
  irregular 64

Part-time work 74, 84, 101
  at home 85
  Supplementary Benefit 84
Payments
  door-to-door collection of 53, 56, 150, 169
  frequent demands for 58
  missing payments 75
  repayment programme 169
Personal Bond (Scotland) 204
Personal Loan 22, 26
Poinding (Scotland) 202, 203
  exempt goods 202, 203
Post Office 86, 88, 108, 110, 140, 170
Prescriptions
  as an essential outgoing 113
  free 88, 103
Priority debt 121, 131, 136, 147, 149, 150
  definition of 123, 151
  sanctions for 123, 147, 192
Protected earnings level 189

Rates, see also Water Rates 65, 86, 87, 105, 133
  rebate 86, 133
  how to pay 109
Rates Arrears 132, 133, 134, 135
  distraint 123, 132, 133
  final sanction 123, 132
  how to calculate payment 133
  imprisonment 132, 133
  in Scotland 204
Rebates
  for early settlement of credit 73
  rates 86, 133
  rent 86, 130
Red-lining 38
Repayment Programme 156, 173
  consequences of reducing payments 170, 171
  creditors accept 162
  creditors refuse 158, 162, 166

  how to draft 156
  interest and 159
  no disposable income 171
  use in Court proceedings 167
  ways of paying 169, 170
Rent 86, 87, 105
  fair rent registration 130
  how to pay 109
  rebate 86, 130
Rent arrears 86, 130, 131, 132
  administration orders 190, 191
  direct payment by DHSS 131
  distraint 123, 131, 132
  eviction 123, 130, 182
  final sanction 123, 131–2
  housing benefit 130
  possession summons 131, 179
Revolving credit 20, 32, 158
  definition of 20
  interest and 21
Running Credit Account
  definition of 20

Second mortgage 72, 73, 105, 124, 125, 129
  arrears 123, 124, 127
  Court proceedings 124, 127, 129
  early settlement of 73, 125
  income tax 80, 125
Seizure Order (Northern Ireland) 197, 198
Self Employed
  essential outgoings 111
  income of 63
  priority debts of 147
Sheriffs Court, see also Court system in Scotland 199, 200, 201, 203, 204, 205, 217
Shop credit 23
Small Business Advisory Service 147
Social Fund 89
Solicitor 91, 177, 180, 182, 194
  debt passed to 177
  and legal aid 91, 117, 145
  when to consult 91, 194

Staff Welfare funds 96, 101
Students 90, 98
    covenants 98
Summons
    default 184
    fixed date 182, 183
    in Northern Ireland 197
    possession 179
    responding to 179, 186
Supplementary Benefit 87, 88–9,
    95, 100, 125, 136, 139
    abolition of 89
    claiming 87
    fuel direct 141, 142
    living on 87, 119
    low wages 83
    part-time work 84
    rent arrears direct 131
    single payments 88

Tax
    see Income Tax
    see VAT
Telephone 65, 117, 155, 156
Television 65
    as an essential outgoing 65, 106,
    108
    licence 106, 108
Time Orders 193
    applying for 193
Trade Unions
    low wages 83, 101
Trading down 74

Trading Standards
    Department 57
    Officer 43
Travelling Expenses 65
    as an essential outgoing 65, 104,
    105, 107, 108
Trustee in Bankruptcy 207

Unemployment 82, 84, 86, 87, 95,
    172, 175
Unemployment Benefit 89, 136
Unsecured Credit 29, 30, 156

VAT 64, 81, 123, 147
Video 65, 104, 116, 117

Wages, see also earnings 83
    low 79, 82, 83, 84, 86
    arrestment of 201, 202
    attachment of 95, 188, 189, 193
Wages Council Orders 83
    minimum wages 83
Walking possession 187, 195
Warrant of Execution 187
    exempt goods 187
    suspension of 188
Warrant of Possession 182
    suspension of 182
Warrant of Recovery 183
Warrant Sale (Scotland) 202, 203
Water Rates 87, 105
    arrears 123, 135
    payment of 109, 135
Writing off debts 135